The
SEVEN
PEOPLE
PRINCIPLES
Success When Dealing
With Other People
CUBIE DAVIS KING, PhD.

The 7 People Principles
Success When Dealing With Other People

King Publishing

Dr. King's books are available at special quantity discounts
for bulk purchases or sales promotions, premiums, fund raisers,
or educational use.

Special books or book
excerpts can also be created to fit your specific needs.

For details e-mail Dr. King @

cubie@goldcrowninc.com
www.goldcrowninc.com
www.cubieking.com

Other Books by Cubie Davis King, PhD.

HOW TO CALL A MEETING WITH YOURSELF: DAILY
SUCCESS HABITS THAT PRODUCE STUNNING RESULTS

YOU CEO: HOW TO THINK LIKE A CORPORATE BOSS
AND CAUSE YOUR STOCK TO SOAR IN ANY ECONOMY

OPK: OTHER PEOPLE'S KNOWLEDGE: GROW RICH
MIMICKING AND MODELING THE SUCCESSES OF
OTHERS

Dedication

This book is dedicated to those who realize that in order to succeed at the highest levels of society, you must master the art of dealing with people.

To Jennifer
Dream Big!
-DR. King

Table of Contents

The 7 People Principles:

Success When Dealing With Other People

"Dealing with people is the biggest problem you face. A person's ability to understand and get along with people... and actually win others to their way of thinking is key to moving up in today's' organizations."

-Dale Carnegie

"To be successful in the workplaces of today-you must master the art of listening, become proficient at resolving conflicts, become a point person for orchestrating cooperation among employees, and develop a leadership style that inspires others. In other words you must manage emotions with intelligence.

-Cubie Davis King

"Market forces are reshaping our work life and putting an unprecedented premium on intelligence for on-the-job success"

-Daniel Goleman

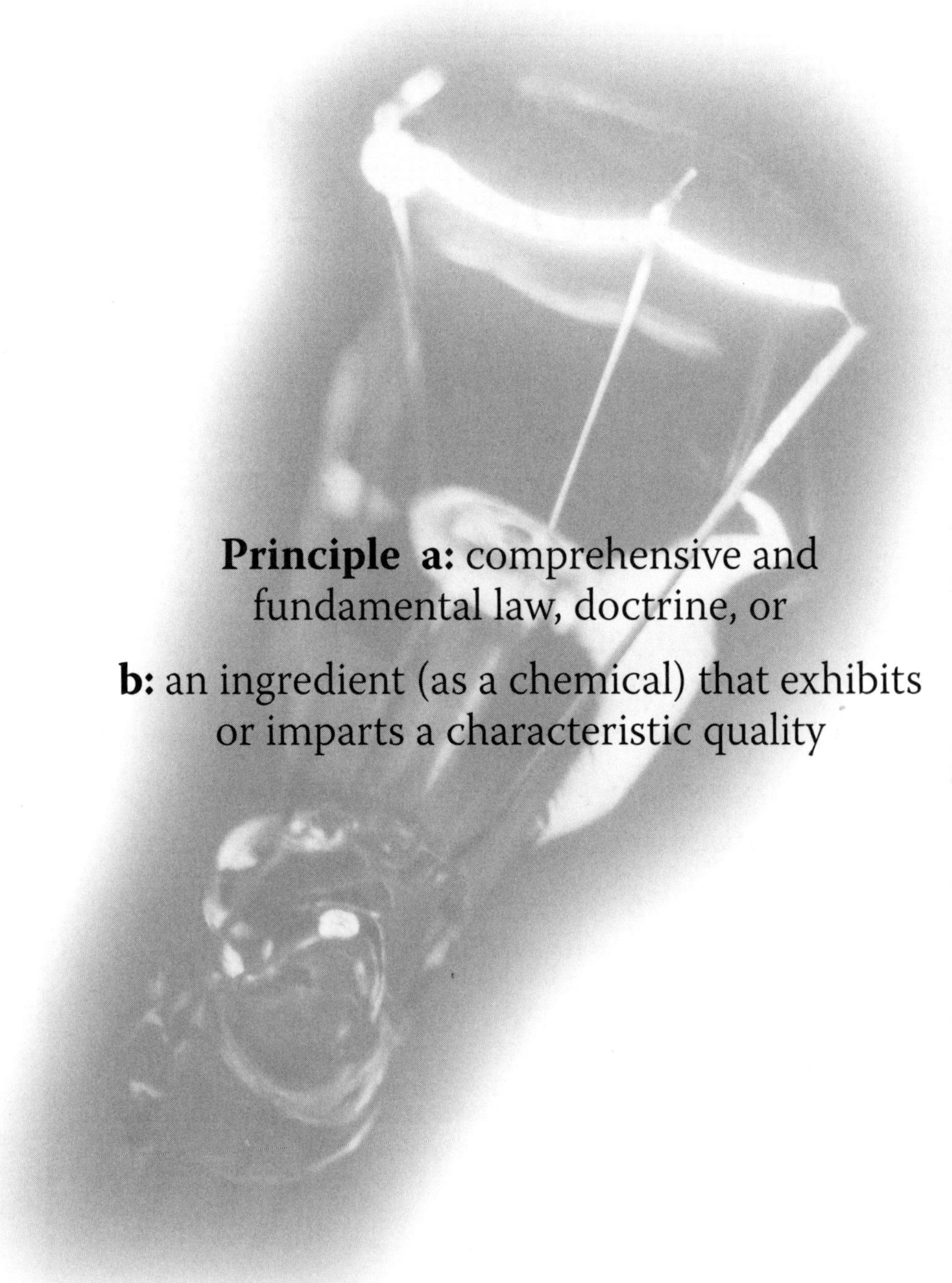

Principle a: comprehensive and fundamental law, doctrine, or

b: an ingredient (as a chemical) that exhibits or imparts a characteristic quality

CHAPTER ONE

People Principle Number 1

People Want To Feel Special

Over time, people may forget your name and they may even forget the way you look; but people never forget the way you make them feel.

- Author Unknown

Lesson from Grade School

Let me use your imagination for a moment and take you back to elementary school. For most of us those were happy days, where we first learned to play with our friends and to get along with others. We discovered that we were not the only ones who wanted to play with the toys in the toy box. There were other kids who wanted to play as well; so we had to learn to share.

I remember recess time when the bell rang and all the kids ran out onto the playground to play any number of sports. Team captains were named and given the opportunity to choose the kids they wanted to play on their teams. Remember how great it felt when you were chosen to play on one of those teams? You felt special. How about when your classmates asked you to trade something from your lunch with them? How special you felt when they chose you as a trading partner. Or when a teacher singled you out as having the best coloring project in the class? Once again you felt special. In each of these cases there was something dynamic at work; we experienced being made to feel special. Stay with me because I'm leading up to the first people principle.

Now for a moment, I want you to imagine any number of special feelings you experienced as a child growing up in grade school and high school. Think about those pep rallies, science fairs, Friday night football games, cheerleading, parades, music classes, gymnastics, and more. Wow, do you remember how special you felt?

Memories Are Powerful

I remember in the sixth grade hearing a group on the radio playing one of my favorite songs entitled *"what does it take to win your love for me"* and how I was instantly smitten with a burning desire to play the saxophone. The group's name was Jr. Walker & The All Stars. I ran to my mom and told her I just had to play saxophone. So my mother scraped together every penny she could muster and signed a lease agreement to get my first saxophone. How special I felt.

By the time I reached the seventh grade I was one of five music protégés selected (by our high school band director, Mr. Warner) to play in the advanced band; an honor, up and until then, was reserved only for sophomores, juniors, and seniors. I felt very special then. And until this day, some 40 years later, I yet carry around that special feeling and time in my life as a memorial of appreciation to Mr. Jerry Warner of Dallas, Texas.

People Never Forget

I'm going to say something I hope you never forget. In fact you should print it out so you can see it everyday of your life. I can't remember exactly where or who I heard this from, but it goes something like this;

Over a long period of time, people may forget your name, and people may even forget the way you look; but people never forget the way you make them feel.

-Anonymus

Now read it again, but this time read it slowly.

I'm sure when you look back on your life you can remember moments in your like where you felt extra special. Then there are those moments in our lives we'd all like to forget. For example (think for a moment), we all can remember that one boss in our life that pressured us unnecessarily, dealt with us harshly, or judged us unfairly? Yeah, that one! Even after many years, you've never forgotten how that person made you feel.

The Job Satisfaction Survey

In 1987 The Conference Board (www.conference–board.org), a global, independent business membership and research association began tracking employee job satisfaction. Their 1987 research revealed that nearly 61% of American workers were satisfied with their jobs. By 2009 (twelve years later) that number had dropped precipitously to only 45%. That's a 55% negative rating, the lowest level since it started tracking these data.

Figure 1. The Jobs Satisfaction Survey
Source: The Conference Board

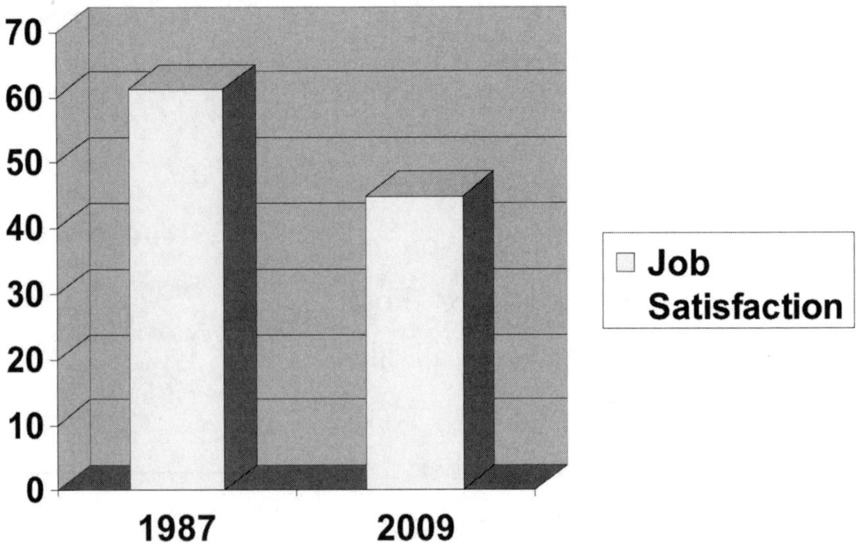

Those Most Dissatisfied

In the 2009 survey, the age groups least satisfied with their jobs were those under the age of 25 years old. One may argue it's because this age group is often just getting started in the workplace, and chances are they are in relatively low paying jobs that they would like to get out of. And this may be a valid argument. However, significant in the study's findings was the revelation that those workers over the age of 35 years old also expressed a high degree of dissatisfaction with their jobs. In a global economy where American businesses must now compete in world markets, many believe this high degree of job satisfaction among workers over the age of 35 may be an eerie harbinger of serious problems ahead for American employers.

People Skills Will Be Key

Therefore, your people skills will matter even more in the workplaces of the future. It's not hard to imagine why the productivity rates of employees go down - when high job dissatisfaction rates are up. This can have a negative impact on the bottom line profits of any company, and become a nightmare for leaders. In fact, according to the 2011 edition of The Conference Board CEO Challenge, a survey where some 704 top CEOs, presidents, and chairmen across the globe responded to questions asking them to identify the most critical challenges facing their organizations, the vast majority said that business growth is the greatest challenge their organizations face.

However, according to the Conference Board, in order for companies to achieve business growth in the future, they will need to concentrate on three distinct areas:

(1) Have a clear vision for where the company is heading.

(2) Have strong and thoughtful visionary leadership and,

(3) Have high performance teams who have learned to work together.

In other words, businesses will need talent with impeccable people skills.

Your Greatest Challenge in Life

Anyone who has ever attempted to lead a team of people will attest to the fact that the greatest challenge you'll face as the leader is getting those individuals (with their own independent ways of thinking) to work together as a team. In fact Dale Carnegie, author of the all time best seller on how to deal with humans- entitled "How to Win Friends and Influence People," wrote this:

"Dealing with people is the biggest problem you face. A person's ability to understand and get along with people... and actually win others over to their way of thinking is key to moving up in today's organizations."

-Dale Carnegie

Interestingly enough, Dale Carnegie wrote those words in 1936, but they are as true today as they were then.

Someone said, "If it wasn't for the people I have to work with, I really could enjoy my job." Humans are fickle individuals who need constant care. They love you in the morning and then hate you in the afternoon.

The Secrets of the Ages

This book, *The 7 People Principles: Success When Dealing With Other People* - will help you master the art of working with others. Page, after eye opening page unearths those forgotten secrets and principles that helped men and women of old rise to the top of their industry.

Your First Lesson

The first lesson to remember when dealing with people is this: everyone wants to feel important, and be a part of something special. From the janitor to the chief executive everyone has an innate desire to have their life count for something. This is why people join clubs, sororities, fraternities, churches, synagogues, teams, acting clubs, and other associations. Why - because they want to feel needed and respected.

The workplaces of today are no different. People want to know that they are needed and that their contributions matter to the organization. I believe the reason we see so much dissatisfaction in the workplaces of today is people just don't know how, and where, they fit in their organizations. What I've found in life is this; it's hard to get excited about something you don't understand. With a 55% dissatisfaction rate in the workplaces of today, a central part of the job of today's leaders is to stir the pot, create some excitement, and make people feel they are a part of something special. In other words make them feel they are back at one of those special events they experienced in school.

Excitement Wins

I remember attending an annual convention of a Fortune 500 company some twenty-five years ago that I'll never forget. I walked into this huge auditorium where close to 60,000 employees were standing on their feet. The company had upbeat music playing loudly, and the employees were dancing and having a great time. And why not, they had just beaten one of the top companies in their industry and taken over the number two spot.

When the CEO came out on stage the thunder of the employees' was deafening. This guy was like a rock star. And then he spoke. Instantly I understood why the company was so successful. The leader was excited and exciting to watch. The last time I got a feeling like this was back in high school at those Friday pep rallies, just before the big game. He made everyone in that room feel important as he told them that each and everyone ones' contributions counted toward them taking over the number two spot. That day, even I felt special - like I was a part of this special group of people - even though I was a visitor. On that particular day I learned a valuable lesson about dealing with people - EXCITEMENT WINS!

Observe For Yourself

Can you name one team in any sport that wins their national championship and everyone is moping around with frowns on their faces? No, not one! Everyone is jumping up and down, yelling, screaming, running, and high fiving each other while they celebrate their great achievement.

Fifty per cent of winning at anything in life is being excited. What a shame that the majority of companies have lost the very excitement on which they were founded. The excitement that caused the original founders of the company to come to work early and stay late. Not because they had to, but because they wanted to. Why - because they believed they were building something special.

Still Children at Heart

In so many ways, we are all still children at heart. We still want to be the person chosen to be apart of a special team. That little kid inside of us is jumping up and down yelling, "me, me, choose me." And that kid is saying, "coach if you choose me you will never regret it, because I will work hard in helping the team to succeed." The sad fact for most organizations is the excitement is gone. Everyday people come to workplaces around the world looking like zombies, and working like robots with no heart or feelings.

Show People You Care

Listen, you can act like you care about people, but sooner or later people will find you out. You see, people can smell a phony a mile away. And if people ever feel that you are not genuinely interested in their well being, they will stop giving their best efforts.

Conversely, when people feel that you care and they can see this in your eyes, hear it in your voice, and see it in your actions, they will give a dedication to their work that will amaze you, and help push the team to victory. Show people that you care and make them feel special and they will help you succeed.

What I Was Happy To Witness

Recently I was invited to Texas to speak to a group of managers at a very successful food distribution company. When I arrived at this very large facility I was amazed at what I witnessed firsthand. From the moment I walked through the doors everyone was smiling and greeting each other. Now, they didn't know me, so they could not be faking this, because everyone acted the same. No this was deeply embedded in their organization's culture.

As I walked down this long corridor to the meeting room where I was to speak, I could tell the people were alive, alert and excited to be on the job. As I waited to speak to this crowd of about 150 managers, I keenly watched and observed how the employees conversed with each other. I could tell they really enjoyed being with one another. No, this was not a "put on," - this was real. I know because I have been in enough settings (business, civic, even religious) where people were gathered over the last 40 years (including my nine years serving in the military, four years in government, twelve years as a corporate executive, and fifteen years as a corporate trainer) to know the difference between something real and something fake. Let me say again - this was real.

Look To The Top

While I was speaking, the CEO walked in and sat amongst the managers. During the break I was introduced to him and instantly understood why this group of 150 leaders acted with such excitement and professionalism. The CEO had a personality that instantly won you over. He had a flair for making people feel special. There is absolutely no doubt in my mind that he has mastered and thoroughly understands this first people principle which is: everyone wants to feel special. This amazing company was number one in their market, and this once again confirmed for me that companies who make their people feel special (like the Fortune 500 company I mentioned earlier), seem to dominate their industries. Wow, I wish I really could put into words what I experienced that day. Incidentally, while I was up speaking, I told them that they had something special there and to never let it slip away. Now, let me tell you about my experience from the other side.

What I Wish I Hadn't Witnessed

On another occasion I was invited to speak at a major electronic manufacturing concern on the west coast. I idolized this company and had purchased some of their products, so I really looked forward to my visit. I was there to conduct training for around 30 managers. I arrived at the company early (as is my custom) so I could observe the employees as they arrived for work. Part of my job as a performance technologist is to study people. And it doesn't take me long to get a feel for how a company operates. I simply watch its employees. The one thing I noticed right away, was that there was a lack of excitement, as I watched employee after employee enter the building.

After passing through security, I was escorted to the meeting room where the training was to be held. I set up my equipment and had at least 45 minutes before the meeting was to begin. Through a glass door I could see employees walking around as their day began. Unlike the other company I talked about earlier, there was something missing. I asked to use the restroom and as I passed down the hall not one single person said hello. There were no smiles or friendly greetings. Right then and there, I knew I was in for a long day.

My Suspicions Were Confirmed

When the time came for the meeting, I watched as one manager after another dragged in late (some as late as half an hour). There was very little excitement or enthusiasm in the room, and all during the training some of the managers walked in and out throughout the entire day's training. It took me less than a half a day to understand why this company had lost its competitive edge in the market place. This company used to be number one in their field, but not anymore. The thrill was gone.

Honestly, I couldn't wait to get out of there. The atmosphere in that place was poisoned with negativity and I don't know anyone who is able to perform at their highest level of productivity for long in such an environment. Folks, just like enthusiasm is contagious, so too is negativity.

I often say, give me a little time with the leader of the organization and I'll describe for you the team. On the other hand, give me a little time with the team, and I'll describe for you the leader.

-Cubie Davis King

Your Mental DNA

Clearly demonstrated in the two case studies I talked about earlier (i.e. the food distribution company and the electronics manufacturing company), is the fact that people take on the mental DNA (or mentality) of their leader. Enthusiasm and a cultural of respect must begin with the leader, however, it can also become contagious from the bottom up. There is a reason why leader companies such as Apple, StarBuck's, Subway, and Wal-Mart dominate their markets. Take a look at the culture of these organizations and you'll find at its roots excitement, enthusiasm, and a workforce that is made to feel special. This is no accident.

We're Number One

What is the first thing you hear when you enter a Subway Restaurant? The very same thing I heard some 15 years ago when I dined at one for the first time in San Diego, CA; "Welcome to Subway." The culture of the people who serve you is friendly and polite. Where do you suppose this winning attitude comes from? I'm willing to bet it emanates directly from the top. How great is the culture at Subway Sandwiches? Well today, as of this writing, Subway is the largest single-brand restaurant chain in the world, now surpassing McDonald's. And folks you don't get to beat an organization like McDonald's on a whim, you beat them on strategy! And one of those strategies is to create a culture where people are made to feel special.

What is the first thing you hear when you enter a Wal-Mart? "Welcome to Wal-Mart." Again this is no accident. These companies have created a culture of enthusiasm, and like a football, baseball, hockey, or basketball team when the momentum shifts their way - they are hard to beat!

People Are Like Mirrors

Let me ask you a question. When people approach you on a personal level, what greeting are you sending out? Are you sending out a hearty welcome - or is it a nasty, "get away from me." People can tell right away because people are like mirrors which simply reflect the image it sees.

In the very same way, people reflect back to you the attitude you give to them. If you are nasty to them, they have a tendency to be nasty to you. On the other hand, when you are polite and respectful to them, they have a tendency to mirror that attitude and be nice and respectful to you.

Here is a saying that may seem corny but it is absolutely true: "Smile; and the world smiles with you." When you pass people and smile, they, more often than not, will smile right back at you. Let me reiterate: People are like mirrors, they simply reflect your attitude toward them. Now, let's bring in some empirical data. What we are talking about is making people feel special.

Case #1

During a human development study conducted by Dale Carnegie (How To Win Friends and Influence People), he asked thousands of businessmen to smile at someone every hour of the day for one week and then report their findings back to him. The results were absolutely stunning. People reported that their lives were changed forever. Many reported that they were happier at home, and many others reported that business had picked up tremendously. From home to office many were empowered to new heights of greatness - all because of a smile.

Case #2

Napoleon Hill, in his run-away best seller *"Think & Grow Rich"* gives an account of a company during the Great Depression which, despite the stock market crash, not only survived but thrived, even with businesses failing all around them. Their secret: The owner affixed a large mirror on the back of each sales truck, and instructed his salespeople not to call on one client until they could look in that mirror, smile, and first convince themselves they could make the sale. They killed their competition.

Case #3

In 1974, I served on the USS Denabola (our ship carried food to the fleet). I remember on one deployment (the ship going to sea), that the attitudes of the crew, for one reason or another, were absolutely rotten. Perhaps it was because we were directed to go to sea on three back-to-back tours; meaning we were in port for only four weeks before we had to leave again. Many of my shipmates had families at home (I was single at the time). No matter, attitudes were stinky. A fistfight broke out on the ship everyday for about the first four weeks. Well, it was purported that the Captain (after getting reports of these fights) called all the senior enlisted officers of every department on the ship together and instructed them to smile, and have their people smile at each other as they carried out their duties throughout the day. What I remember most about this experience is how weird it felt the first few days. The same people smiling at you everyday. Remember, we are sailors at sea. By the end of the first week of this experiment, those bad attitudes had lifted and, believe it or not, people began to expect a smile from others. What an incredible experience.

A smile is the universal language of winners. It is an instant door opener. Show me a person who has mastered it, and I'll show you a person hovering at the top of the most powerful organizations in the world. The psychology behind it is absolutely stunning.

-Cubie King

People won't follow a bitter, frustrated old crybaby.

-Art Williams

A person is ultimately responsible for the condition of their face.

-Abraham Lincoln

Was our Captain a genius? Perhaps, but one thing is for certain, he had a keen understanding of this first people principle - and that people are like mirrors, simply reflecting the attitudes they are given. The Captain used this knowledge to inspire his crew to greatness.

The following poem sums up the power of a simple smile:

The Psychology of a Smile

It cost nothing, but creates much. It enriches those who receive, without impoverishing those who give. It happens in a flash and the memory of it sometimes lasts forever. None is so rich they can get along without it, and none so poor but are richer for its benefits. It is rest to the weary, daylight to the discouraged, sunshine to the sad, and Nature's best antidote for trouble. Yet it cannot be bought, begged, borrowed, or stolen, for it is something that is no earthly good to anybody until it is given away.

-Frank Irving Fletcher

One of the greatest ways to make people feel special instantly is to offer them a smile.

Conduct - An Honest Assessment

Look around your organization.

1. Have your team leaders lost their enthusiasm?

2. Do your people still feel special - and Do they feel are a part of something special?
3. What person on the team brings the most excitement?
4. How can your organization tap into this enthusiasm and build something fresh and new from this excitement?

Remember, 50% of winning is being excited! And never forget, everyone wants to be a part of something special.

1. What knowledge from this chapter can you pass on to your leaders and managers about dealing with employees and teams? Write your answers here.

____

____

____

____

____

____

____

____

Don't stop now. The excitement continues in Chapter 2 where I reveal the forgotten secret of why employees today have lost that excitement; and how your organization can get it back almost instantly. So quick, let's go on to People Principle #2...

People Principle #1

People Want To
Feel Special!

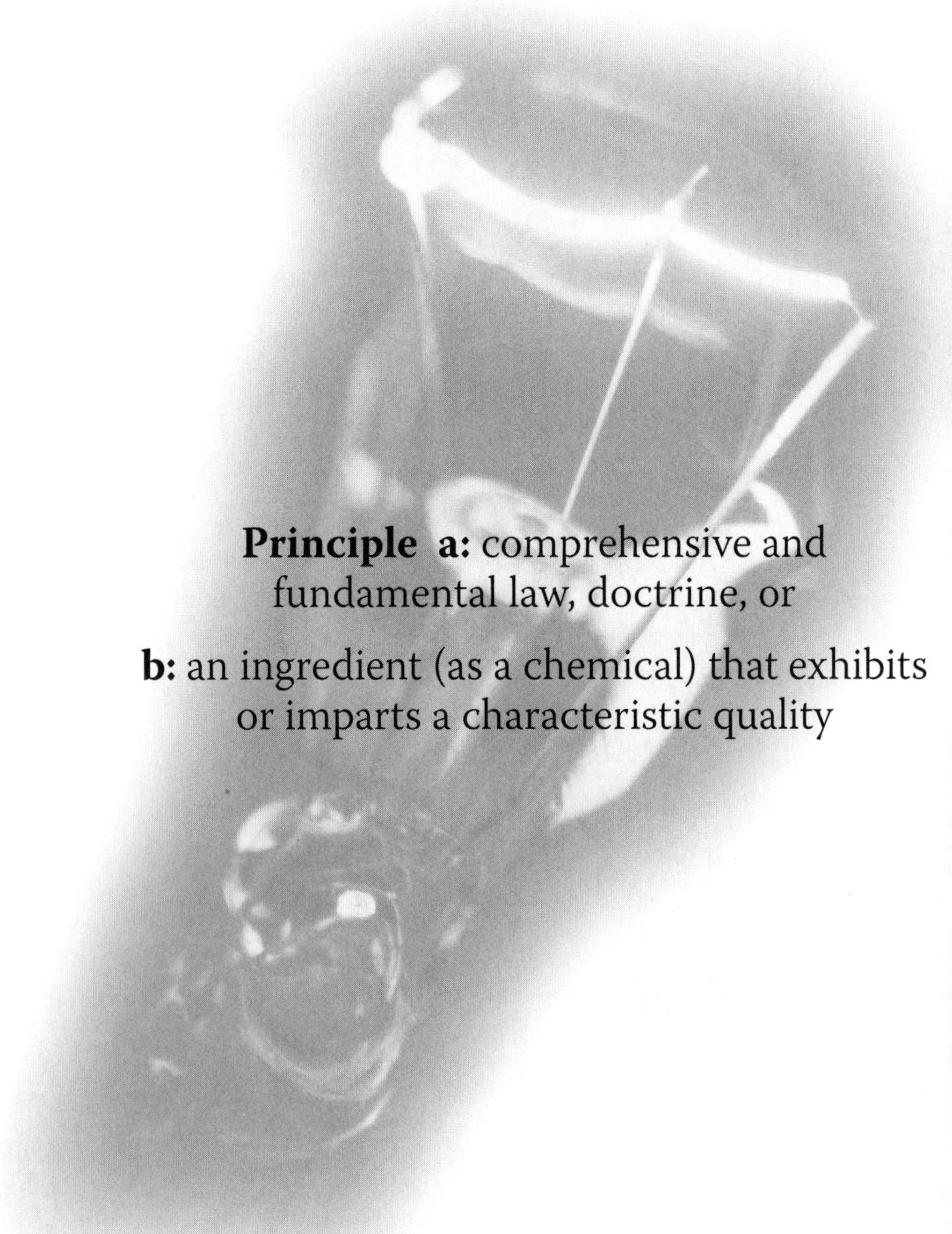

Principle a: comprehensive and fundamental law, doctrine, or

b: an ingredient (as a chemical) that exhibits or imparts a characteristic quality

CHAPTER TWO

People Principle Number 2

People Want Clear Directions

It's hard to get excited about something You don't understand.

-Cubie Davis King

This Changed Everything

It happened when I was a young sailor just twelve months into my naval career. This near death experience shook me at my very core and changed my life forever. Aboard the USS Denabola (a refrigerated cargo ship which carried food and supplies to ships at sea) is where I served as a storekeeper in the supply department.

Life was good, as I actually was living my dream of "Join the Navy and see the world." The only problem was the Navy seemed to get in the way of me "seeing the world." Day after day we put in long grueling hours, as ship after ship pulled along side our ship to receive food and supplies. Then, as if those long hours were not enough, the Captain of the ship would have these "preparation to anything" drills in the middle of the night. The navy called them general quarters drills. How insensitive of the Captain I thought. Didn't he know I had just gotten in my rack (bed for you land lovers) and barely had fallen off to sleep? Well, apparently not. I can't recall how many of these unexpected drills we had in the middle of the night, and at different times of the day before it happened.

What Happened?

In one split second, life aboard the USS Denabola would change dramatically. While replenishing a giant aircraft carrier with food and supplies in the dead of night, with only the moon for light, the Captain sensed something was wrong with the way both ships were aligned. The situation quickly spun out of control as these two ships (steaming along side each other) rocked back and forth toward each other.

With the intent of avoiding a collision with this big aircraft carrier, the Captain yelled to the quartermaster on deck "right full rudder!" The situation was extremely tense. And in a panic the quartermaster on deck, spun the wheel left full rudder. And with a boom I thought could be heard around the world, we hit that big gray beast.

I was on deck as our ship shook violently, like a child playing with a toy in the bathtub. Everyone fell to the deck and held on for dear life. It all seemed like a movie being played in fast forward. Both ships seemed out of control as we braced for another hit. Then a brave Master Chief Petty Officer, with nearly thirty years of experience being at sea, came running down the deck yelling, "everybody get out of the way, get out of the way" The reason he was yelling at us to get out of the way was because the cables (or whips) which are used to transport cargo between ships, had snapped off and were slithering down the deck like angry snakes out for revenge. These whips have the capability of instantly cutting off a person's head or limb, like a hot knife going through butter. You could literally hear the whipping sound as these huge cables (four of them) slithered down the deck.

The collision cut a long gapping hole in our ship as easy as someone taking a can opener to an aluminum can. The ship immediately began taking on water. Well, when you're in the middle of the ocean you can't call a plumber - we were the plumbers. Fires broke out in several compartments. We couldn't call the fire department - we were the fire department. Many of my ship mates were injured. It was beyond frightening. I said my prayers because I honestly thought we were going to die. There was no way we could swallow all of that water in the middle of the ocean.

Pay Close Attention to the Mission

Then, as if by a miracle, the Captain regained control of the ship. We immediately went to general quarters (you know - those drills I and most of my shipmates hated the Captain for, because he conducted them at all times of the day and night). I watched in absolute amazement as each of my shipmates carried out the very duties the Captain had us rehearse those many times.

There were those who plugged the hole in the ship so we wouldn't sink. There were others who put out the fires so we wouldn't burn. And there were medics who tended to those who were hurt during the ordeal. It looked like something out of a movie - but it was real! I can honestly say, watching my shipmates perform their duties and saving our ship, was one of the proudest moments of my naval career. You see, what we were practicing during all those drills was a vital part of the mission of the ship; only at the time (I was 18 years old) and I didn't understand that fact.

This Changed Me Forever

This near death experience changed my view of life in the military, and life in general, forever. Because of that collision, our ship had to be towed to Spain to be repaired. This gave me a lot of time to reflect on what had happened, and I realized just how close we came to death. This was no joke. I realized for the first time that I was working with real professionals;

people who knew their jobs and did them well. For the first time I felt proud to be in the United States Navy.

I Made Some Major Changes

When the whole experience finally hit me, I made up my mind right then to make some major changes in my life. Thinking of the heroics of my shipmates and how they had saved my life; I decided to make a commitment to excellence in everything I do from that day forward. I thought if I could depend on my shipmates in a life or death situation like that, they ought to be able to depend on me.

From that day to this (some 37 years later) I have put forth my best efforts in every job I have held in my life. And from that very day, at every single place I have worked during my entire career, I have won the organization's top performance awards. What drives me? In part, the memory of that infamous day.

Why the Mission Matters

You see, after that experience I began to inquire and pay close attention to the mission of the ship (what we were trying to accomplish). After finding that out, it became easier for me to get excited about playing my part in accomplishing our mission. I was so driven, that within months, I was named "sailor of the quarter." Therefore, if you want people to get excited about working with you, no matter what you are trying to accomplish, your mission has to be clear in the minds and hearts of your people.

rill is Gone

One of the unwritten laws of the workplace is that it's hard to get excited about something you don't understand. I believe this is the reason we see so many people today who have little or no excitement in the workplace. Day after day thousands of people go to places they absolutely dread. You see it when you go for breakfast in the morning, take your lunch break in the afternoon, and wind down for dinner at night. Unhappy people, working at unhappy places, doing unhappy work, earning incomes they are unhappy with. People acting like robots, just going through the motions. Just thinking about it makes you sad, doesn't it?

Well It Doesn't Have To Be

Do you want to get employees excited about work again? Then help them to *clearly* understand the mission of the company. Then take the next power step in the process: help them understand exactly how they fit into this mission. It's hard *not* to get excited when you know your contributions count at work. And that you are recognized for those achievements which have a direct impact in accomplishing the mission of the organization.

Every Level Counts

On every level of the organization you must paint a clear picture for your people, of where the organization is heading and what it hopes to accomplish. From the top to the bottom, everyone on every level must be assured that they count.

For example: in the restaurant business, the best measurement of how well that business is operated is not the splendid ocean view, or gorgeous sunsets you can enjoy while dining, or the breath-taking ambience and décor of the restaurant. No, the best indicator of how well that business is managed is found in its restrooms. If the restrooms are filthy, chances are other areas of the restaurant are filthy. And who uses those same restrooms besides you and those other patrons; your server. So how can having a clean restroom fit into the overall mission of the company?

The CTP Formula

As a leader of that business, I'd have all employees understand why those restrooms must be kept clean. I'd explain to my staff that an important part of our mission is for customers to feel we are the premier place to come when they have a taste for say; Italian, Chinese, Greek, American, Korean, or Soul Food (whatever the restaurant serves). And being a premier restaurant includes cleanliness in all areas. I'd get every employee to understand that clean restrooms demonstrate to our customers on a daily basis, our commitment to achieving this mission.

Finally, I'd help all employees understand the CTP (customer-to-paycheck) formula for success which equates to this: if our customers stop coming through those doors, we all stop getting a paycheck. Helping employees understood this simple but powerful concept is worth gold, especially in today's competitive business environment.

How Do I Fit In?

I often make an interesting offer to students attending my seminars. I offer to give a free gift to anyone who can quote (verbatim) the mission statement of their company. In the sixteen years that I have been a corporate trainer how many of these special gifts do you suppose I've had to give out? 1,000, 500, 250? No, zero. Not once has anyone been able to quote verbatim the mission statement of their organization - not one time.

Here are a couple of million dollar questions I want you to ponder.

1. How are employees going to accomplish the mission of the company if they don't understand what the mission is?
2. How can leaders expect employees to get excited about what they don't know, understand, or even recall.

The Million Dollar Answer

The short answer to these questions is they can't. Folks, with every chance you get, remind your people of what your organization is trying to accomplish. Paint a picture, no paint a detailed picture of where the business is heading, what it will look like when you get there, and how special everyone will feel when the mission is accomplished. Help everyone on the team to clearly understand the mission, then add in principle number one, and watch the sparks begin to fly. How important is knowing the mission? Well examine the following case.

His Multi-Million Dollar Mission

He was a giant among men - yet he stood only 5 feet, 3 inches tall. During the late 1800's he amassed over $500,000,000 (five hundred million dollars) in an industry he knew little about. Imagine what that would be worth in today's dollars. Wait a minute. How does a man make that much money in an industry he knows very little about? Well, while he may have known little about the steel business, Andrew Carnegie mastered the art of how to deal with people. He was a master at getting others to see a vision of what he wanted accomplished.

Why is his story so legendary? Because before Andrew Carnegie came along steel was to that era what gold is to us today. It was extremely expensive. In fact, it was so expensive in the early to late 1800's that only the superrich could afford to have things made of steel. It was a high end luxury item.

America Needed Lots of Steel

If America was to grow, to expand, and to build things such as; railroads, buildings, cars, airplanes, washing machines, ships and other things needed to build a powerful and strong nation, it needed steel and tons of it. Steel had to be massed produced. Andrew Carnegie was keen enough to understand this need. So he gathered together a group of powerful investors and painted for them a detailed picture of the America he envisioned.

He helped those investors to clearly understand the mission he was embarking on, which was, for the first time in history, to lower the price of steel for the masses. He helped everyone not only understand that mission, but to believe in the mission.

Remember this, if you want your people, your wife or husband, your family, your organization, and anyone else in your life to help you accomplish your mission, you've got to make absolutely sure that each and everyone of them understands where you are heading (the mission).

The Mission Helps You Focus

After returning from England in 1872, where he watched an English bullet maker demonstrate a new way to produce steel, he returned to America (Pittsburg, PA) and began to build the largest steel plant in the history of the world (the equivalent of 80 football fields long). Talk about ambition.

He risked everything he and the investors put up. And only months into building, the stock market crashed. He had to go back and borrow more money. Again he paints the picture of success not failure, and reminds everyone of the mission (which was to lower the price of steel so America could grow), and how the mission is greater than one temporary setback. The investors understood and put up more money. He and team Carnegie go back to work.

Then in 1875, just three years later, their investments pay off big time. Team Carnegie is the first ever to mass produce steel. Overnight the price of steel plummets by a whopping 80%. The price goes from $160 a ton to $20 a ton. Building in America explodes and by 1900 annual production output is at eleven million tons making Andrew Carnegie one of the richest men in the world.

The most successful companies in the world are those that clarify their mission and set clear goals." The same is true of successful individuals. They know what they are trying to accomplish, and set clear goals.

-Cubie Davis King

A Constant Reminder

This is why it is so vitally important to constantly remind your people of what your organization is trying to accomplish. I can guarantee you, that in order to build a brand that is recognized worldwide, companies like Facebook, Apple, Wal-Mart, Google, Microsoft, Coke, Pepsi, and Subway (to name a few) have mastered the art of painting a clear picture for employees of what the brand is trying to accomplish.

Create a Mission Map

We know that a picture is worth a thousand words. This is why I've always admired the work of architects. They help their clients envision the finished product by creating a model of the building they are going to erect. We've all seen models and artists' renditions of what a building (i.e., a new hotel, hospital, or restaurant) will look like once it is completed. This is no accident; the mission is clear. We are going to build this building!

Now imagine the overall project manager, who is tasked with making sure all of the subcontractors stay on track and complete the tasks, all the while coming under budget. One of the tools (s)he may find useful is a 'mission map," which allows everyone to view (as it were) a snapshot of what the mission is all about.

Take a look at the Mission Map shown in figure 2. The idea is to create a map which will show employees the mission at a glance. At the core of the map is the primary mission of the company. The ancillary boxes show what departments feed directly into the primary mission. Each department will then have a separate sub-mission map. So on and so forth. Again the idea is to show employees how they fit into the grand scheme of things and get them excited about their roles and responsibilities. Your mission maps can be as simple or elaborate as you choose.

Figure 2: Mission Map for Building New Restaurant.

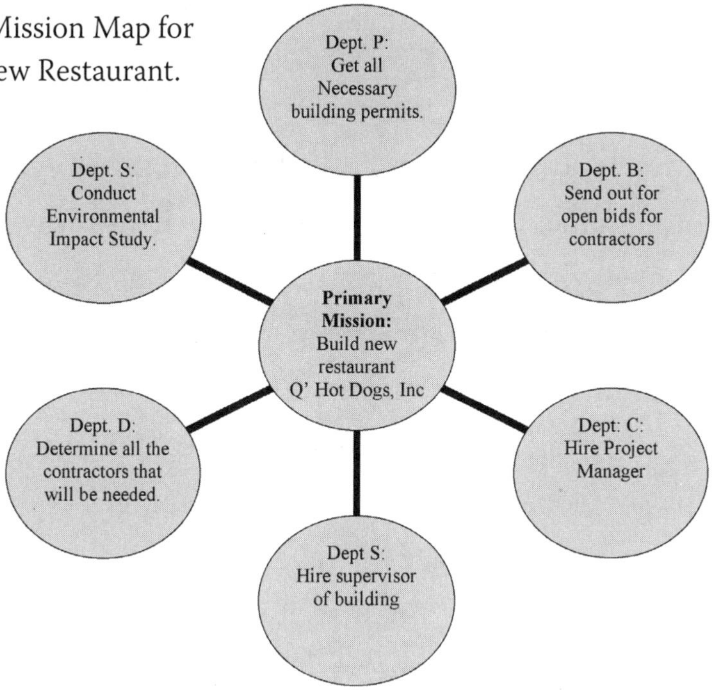

Note: For use as an example only. This particular map is not intended to show any particular order of service or specific steps required to build a restaurant.

No Mission- No Accomplishments

Not long ago I was invited to speak at a major manufacturing concern on the east coast. All of the top managers from around the world including Asia, Europe, South America, and of course North America were at this meeting. Wanting to do a stellar job I researched the company, finding out what products they sold, what their best sellers were, and what new products they were developing. I also went to their web site and reviewed the company's mission statement, which I found to be very inspiring. Armed with this data, I was set to speak at this meeting.

There were around thirty top leaders in attendance along with the CEO, and to kick off the meeting I asked a simple question which turned into a major embarrassment for those in that room. The question I asked was, "can anyone quote the mission statement of the company?" The silence was deafening and seemed to last far longer that the 10 to 15 seconds that I waited for a answer. How many of these top leaders of this major manufacturing concern do you suppose could quote the mission statement of the company? Not one! I thought perhaps someone would, at the very least, get close to what their statement read. Not one even came close. Let me drive home the point once again, that: it is hard to get excited about something you don't understand, let alone accomplish the mission. How are you going to accomplish the mission, if you don't know what the mission is?

Your mission statement should be a brief inspirational message that motivates your team to want to put forth their best efforts toward accomplishing your mission. The mission statement then inspires goal setting from A to Z. You have the overall goal (e.g., to become number one in our market in five years), broken down into yearly goals, then quarterly goals, then monthly goals, then weekly goals, all the way down to a "daily to do list." How do you eat an elephant? One bite at a time. How do you accomplish the mission? One step at a time.

Henry Ford's Impossible Mission

One of the missions Henry Ford (the father of the automobile) set out to accomplish was for the first time, to have eight cylinders on one engine block. In other words, to create the first V-8 engine. He called in his engineers and told them of his idea and they promptly told Mr. Ford that it was impossible to accomplish this mission. Because no one had ever did it. Mr. Ford replied, "yes, yes I know; do it anyway.

Then, Mr. Ford explained in great detail what this mission would mean to the company, the industry, and the world as a whole. He painted a clear picture! The engineers worked tirelessly for six months, nine months, twelve months, and after 18 months those same engineers who said it was impossible, succeeded in creating the first V-8 engine ever produced. They accomplished the mission because the mission was made clear to them by Mr. Ford.

Can You Paint?

One of the greatest people skills you can develop is the ability to paint a clear picture for your team and get them to see a vision of the possibilities. Don't think it strange if you get push-back from employees in the initial stages of the mission. Just keep them focused on what the end product will look like. Be relentless in your pursuit of excellence, and keep them engaged at all times. Help them stay excited about being on your team by reminding them that they play a vital role in accomplishing the mission.

Lessons Learned

1. What knowledge from this chapter can you pass on to your leaders and managers about your mission? Write your answers here: ______________________________

   ____

   ____

   ____

   ____

   ____

   ____.

Now, when you master this next people principle you are almost assured a spot at the top. Let's go directly to Chapter 3 where you'll discover an art form that can literally assure your success...

People Principle #2

People Want Clear Directions

CHAPTER THREE

People Principle Number 3

People Like Listeners!

Give me two people. One who likes to talk and the other who likes to listen- and I'd give the advantage to the listener.

-Cubie Davis King

The Biggest Complaint

What are the greatest complaints employees have about managers and supervisors? They don't listen. What are the greatest complaints people have about salespeople? They don't listen. What is the greatest complaint wives have about their husbands? You guessed it; they don't listen. Listening is the next people principle you must master in order to be successful when dealing with other people. In short, listening is a skill that will get you paid.

Your Visit To The Doctor

You receive a call from your doctor and (s)he asks you to come in immediately to hear the results of a medical test you had done. The results of this test could mean either life or death. While the doctor is talking and explaining the results to you, would you be texting, surfing the internet, eating an apple, or telling the doctor to hurry up because you have a party to go to. No, absolutely not; that is if you have any sense in your head. You'd listen very attentively to every word.

A World Gone Mad?

Take a look at (or listen to) any number of talk shows on the radio and television today and you will see an awful lot of disrespect. People talking, even yelling over each other trying to make their point. And it seems the nastier you are the more points you score. The art of listening to others appears to be fading fast. It's for this very reason those who develop their listening skills will excel in the workplaces of the future.

Don't Under Estimate This Skill

Oprah, one of the richest people on the planet, made her fortune not by being a talk show host, but by listening. People wanted to talk to her because they felt she listened to them. And because she listened, the networks listened and subsequently the world listened.

But it had to go beyond just talk. Oprah had to keenly listen to those businesspeople she was privy to work with. At some point she learned (through the art of listening) how to manage her business affairs and this knowledge propelled her to superstar status. There have been tons of talk show hosts over the years, but none (to date) have excelled like Oprah.

Listeners Have The Advantage

The greatest part of communicating with others is listening. When people talk too much they deprive themselves of the opportunity to learn valuable information from other people. What I've found out, in the half plus century I've been on this earth is, people will help you succeed far beyond your wildest imagination - if you'd learn to listen.

Picture this; a person walks into a world class meeting where some of the best and brightest minds in their industry are gathered. Wanting to impress this group with how much he knows, he talks excessively about himself; and never really gets to know the other people in attendance at this important meeting.

On the other hand, another person, who is also invited to the same meeting walks around getting others to talk about themselves, listens carefully, and shows great interest in what those individuals have to say. Who would you say has the advantage? If you said the listener you are correct. Studies after studies have shown that people who are considered great listeners are also considered great communicators.

How to Get Respected

Isn't it interesting that great listeners are regarded as great communicators. Now I'm talking intelligence, not silliness. If you look at some of those television programs where people are fighting and telling all of their business, then yeah, the loudest person appears to win.

But intelligent professionals who know when to speak and when to listen are revered as great communicators. Someone once said "God gave us two ears and one mouth; so we would spend twice as much time listening as we do talking." Sounds corny, but adhering to this saying could help you move up in your organization.

It's Easy to Win Friends

The easiest way to win friends is to let people talk about themselves. People often dislike going to places where they know few people. I relish it because it's easy to make new friends. Just get people talking about themselves and you will be a hit with everyone. The same holds true in business. Coach Art Williams, the man who built a powerful brand at CitiGroup said in his incredible book *Pushing Up People* that:

> *"Companies spend billions of dollars annually updating their equipment, investing in new technology, leasing building and office space, advertising their products, decorating their stores, and wooing customers, and then hire people who are poor listeners, and people who are*

rude and obnoxious to the customers, literally chasing them away."

Organizations (in similar fashion) lose billions of dollars each year in lost productivity because managers and supervisors have not learned the art of listening. Listen, if you want to ascend to the heights of incredible success in your career, master the art of listening." Do you want others to find you *interesting*? Then you first must be *interested.*

If managers and supervisors would learn to listen more, they'd find that employees can actually help them succeed in accomplishing the mission of the company, in ways they could never have thought of on their own. Employees often know what works and what doesn't work if only given the chance to be heard. So, don't deny them the opportunity to help *you* succeed. Learn to listen!

There is no mystery concerning successful business conversations. Exclusive attention to the person who is speaking to you is paramount. Nothing else is as flattering as that.

-Charles W. Eliot

The W.A.M. Theory

Dale Carnegie, in his all time international best seller *How To Win Friends and Influence People* wrote: "remember, the person you are talking to is a hundred times more interested in themselves and their wants and needs, than they are in you and your problems. A toothache means more to them than a famine in China that kills a thousand people. Think of that the next time you start a conversation."

So the company becomes number one in the industry. So what? Employees could care less. What they are concerned about are their families and how they will survive. Have you listened and learned enough about me to know that my family comes first, even over all of the profits the company can make. The employee is saying, "help me get what I want and I'll help you get what you want." Listen, and show me you care, and I'll help push you to the top.

Every one operates under the W.A.M. theory; which is "What About Me!" We obsess over our own well being. Quotes like Shakespeare's, "to thine own self be true", and Samuel Butler's, "self-preservation is the first law of nature," drives home the W.A.M. theory. Think about this; when you view a group picture, who is the first face you look for in the crowd? Your own!

One Serious Question

As a leader, if you left the organization you are at today, how many people would truly miss you? The problem is most people spend their life trying to impress people and get them interested in the organization or themselves. People - employees, and clients don't care about you; they care about themselves and their own welfare. Stop trying to get people interested in you. You get interested in them and watch performance levels soar!

Use Listening To Your Advantage

In this same fashion, you can use your listening skills to help your team succeed. When you get people going, they like to talk about their favorite subject - themselves. So listen up. Interestingly; when I was an executive at one Fortune 500 company I discovered how to use listening to my advantage. When I went to lunch with team members, I'd listen as they talked about their husbands or wives, their children and the colleges they were attending, their mortgages, their neighborhoods, their parents and just about anything else. I made mental notes of some of them and used the information they had shared with me to inspire them to better performance. And I got good at it!

On one occasion, one of my teammates told me her child was attending a state university in Texas. Because she talked with such passion and admiration for the school, I knew this was important to her. I listened and learned that it was the child's first year, so while shopping one day I bought her daughter a souvenir with the school's logo on it. When I gave it to her, She was ecstatic. Not because of the gift itself (honestly, it cost me less than five bucks), but because I remembered. She returned the favor with a new dedication to her work that showed up in how well she did her job. Talk about performance improvement. I talk more about this phenomenon of getting peak performance level out of your team(s) in People Principle Number 6.

Words to Live By

As a leader, always remember this: people don't care how much you know, until they know how much you care. Another one of those corny sayings right? But it really is true. Why should people care about you, if you don't care about them? Why should people listen to you, if you don't listen to them? Because I said so? No, that won't work in today's workplaces. That went out when they ceased being children. Even if employees do what you "tell" them, you will not get their very best performance. On the other hand, show employees you care by listening to them (even if you don't agree- listen), and they will break the doors down wanting to work hard for you.

It Works

For those who are skeptical as to if this really works, I can assure you it does. For six years I lead a group of professionals at one of the largest financial services companies in the world. I gained a reputation for being fair and being a person that listened to my people. My team won the top performance awards each and every year for six years. Leaders listen. And listeners become leaders.

Listening Made Him Millions

One evening while having beers with his friends in a bar, a guy listened with intent as his buddies, one after another, vehemently complained about caring for their pets. One of them complained that the money he spent taking his dog to the veterinarian was astronomical. Another one complained that the money he spent on pet food almost matched the money he spent on food for himself. Still another complained that he couldn't go on vacation because his pet could not be left along. He would either have to get a sitter, or take the pet with him. Finally, his last buddy complained about the mess his pet leaves around the house. He whined about always having to clean up after his pet, and that he always had to take the pet for a walk, often when he didn't feel like it.

Nothing special - just an ordinary day with his buddies, hanging at the bar, having beers right? Wrong. Not for this one guy. You see he had mastered the art of listening. And while others heard only complaints - he heard the sound of money and saw a vision of success. While listening to his buddies complain about their pets and their challenges he got a million dollar idea.

Listeners Have the Advantage

He told his buddies he was going to create a pet that would never need food or water; a pet that would never need to be walked, and one you would never have to worry about leaving home along, no matter how many weeks you were gone. A pet you'd never have to take to the doctor; in fact a pet that would never have to be cared for in any special way.

His buddies thought he was crazy but on one fateful evening, while *LISTENING* to his buddies, Gary Dahl, came up with the idea for the *"Pet Rock."* A literal rock, which he put eyes on and placed inside a small box, with the words "Pet Rock" inscribed on the outside. The idea he got LISTENING to his buddies made Gary Dahl a multi-millionaire.

Leaders Listen

Let me say once more: leaders listen! And listeners become great leaders. Show me an organization that is winning in their market, and I'll show you leaders that are hard at work perfecting their listening skills with their people. A leader knows how to ask the right questions in order to get the best performance out of people.

Napoleon Hill talked about the years he spent with Andrew Carnegie (the steel tycoon who commissioned him to study the most successful people of that day). What interested me the most was his recollection that Mr. Carnegie never ever told his managers what to do. He would ask them a series of questions which helped guide them to a logical and successful solution to a problem. Napoleon Hill said Andrew Carnegie was a master at asking the right questions, and that he was an ardent listener. This practice of engaging his managers in their work and in the active solutions to their everyday business challenges allowed his company to dominate the steel industry.

There are reasons a company becomes number one. A great portion of those reasons are the skills the company has when it comes to listening to their employees, to their customers, and to their stakeholders.

One Final Point

Do you want to learn something new and exciting? Then master the art of listening! I was recently asked by one of my students "how do you stay abreast of the latest technology, and then make that technology work for you?" Well, this is no accident. I have a saying that goes like this.

> *As long as you want to earn an income for you and your family, you must keep your knowledge on the cutting edge of your industry.*
>
> -Cubie Davis King

What I try to do, at least once a quarter, is to go into a consumer electronics store (e.g. Best Buy) and simply walk the floor, ask questions of the salesperson concerning the latest tools of the trade, and LISTEN. Imagine, I get to learn how the latest technology works for FREE! All I have to do is what? LISTEN. To the listener goes the spoils; ask Gary Dahl.

Lessons Learned

1. What can you learn from Mr. Carnegie's leadership style? Write your answers here:

   ____.

2. What lessons can you learn from Gary Dahl? Write your answers here:

   ____.

3. What knowledge from this chapter can you pass on to your leaders and managers about dealing with employees? Write your answers here:

   ____

____

____

____

____.

Let's keep going because I'm so excited about sharing this next people principle with you that I can hardly wait. Let me give you a little teaser...people are not always whom you suppose- so many people get fooled. Want to know more? Then quick, let's explore this phenomenon together. Go to Chapter 4...

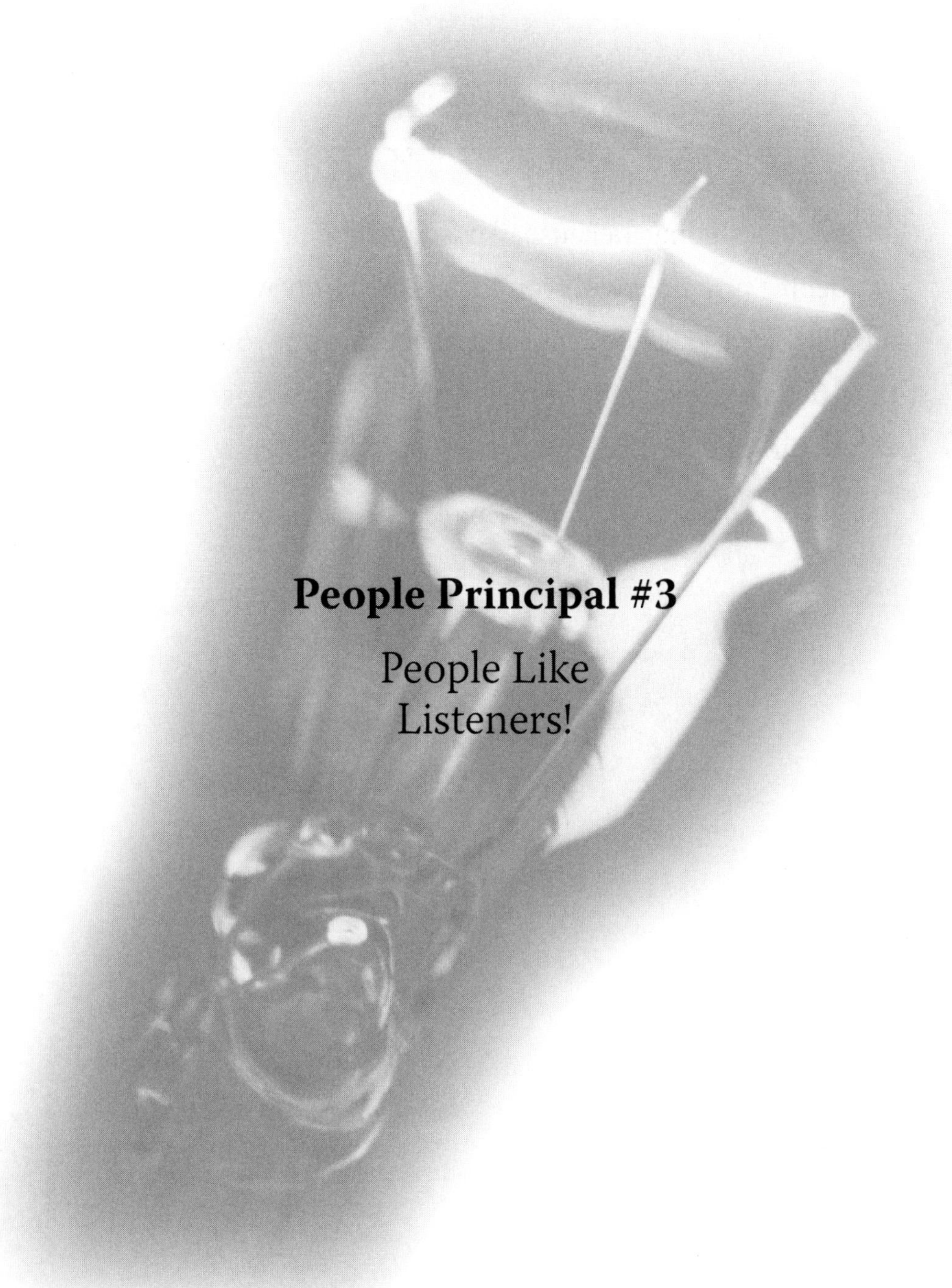

People Principal #3

People Like Listeners!

CHAPTER
FOUR

People Principle Number 4

People Just Want A Fair Chance

There is not a test in the world that can determine in advance those who will succeed or those who will fail in life

-Cubie Davis King

No Test Available

For decades people were judged by how high their IQ was, and how high they scored on aptitude tests. If you had a high IQ, people automatically assumed you would be the leader of the pack and enjoy great success in life. On the other hand, if you had a low IQ, people automatically thought you were in the lowest percentile of humans, and that you would be relegated to the lower rungs of society. How glad I am that studies after studies have proven these hypotheses dead wrong. There has never been a test devised or given (nor will there ever be one devised or given) that can look at a person in their youth and determine how successful they will be in life. Not one.

Here's Proof

Take a look at your high school graduating class. Remember those who were voted most likely to succeed at this or that? Where are they now? Fact is, after twenty plus years most valedictorians and salutatorians are no better off than the average person in their graduating classes. So, the message for you as a leader is this: don't pick your winners too soon. I can't tell you how many times I've been surprised when the person, considered the least likely to succeed, surprised everyone on the team with a stellar performance. Savvy leaders don't discount anyone on their teams because success often comes from unlikely sources and often in unconventional ways.

Empirical Studies Confirm This

Daniel Goleman, author of the incredible book entitled *Emotional Intelligence: Why it can matter more than IQ,* revealed a shocking study conducted in the Illinois school system. Eighty-one valedictorians and salutatorians (those who scored the highest grades in their schools) were followed for ten years after they graduated in 1981. Get this; data showed that while they were tops in their classes, after ten years, only 25% (1 in 4) were at the highest levels of young people in their chosen professions. By their late twenties the majority of them had achieved no more than average success. Wow!

As Karen Arnold, professor of education at Boston University, and one of the researchers of the study said, "to know that a person is a valedictorian is to know only that he or she is exceedingly good at achievement, as measured by grades. It tells you nothing about how they will react to the vicissitudes of life."

That's the Problem

Our society fixates on how smart a person appears to be, however, those of us who have years of life experiences in the workplace know book knowledge does not and cannot fully prepare you for the trials, tribulations and turmoil that the vicissitudes of life brings to everyone. There has never been a test devised that can tell how a person will react to a sudden death in the family, a firing from a job, or how they will react to a overbearing and negative supervisor. Some are able to navigate successfully and work through such difficulties, while others may crash and burn.

There is not a single test that will tell you how happy you will be in life, or in marriage, or how happy you will be on your job. Therefore one must also consider emotional intelligence (EQ). Which some call character or the ability to get along with others, as a factor in how well a person will fare in life.

These Skills Can Be Learned

Goleman wrote, *"much evidence testifies that people who are emotionally adept - who know and manage their own feelings well, and who read and deal effectively with other people's feelings -are at an advantage in any domain in life."* He also believed that people can learn these skills just like, as he said, "learning math or learning to read." This is the exact same conclusion that Dale Carnegie and Napoleon Hill came to over 75 years ago when they wrote their best sellers. So, the good news is: learning the skills necessary to successfully deal with other people, are habits that anyone can learn.

Resumes Are Deceiving

Have you ever hired, worked with, or heard of a person who came to an organization with a stellar resume, great references, and even interviewed well but ended up being a dud instead of a stud? Resumes are like buying stock in companies: "past performance is no guarantee of future performance." Businesses today rely too much on what is on a person's resume, and not on what is in a person's heart.

Recently, in the news, was a report of a internal investigation conducted by the GAO (General Accounting Office) looking into allegations that many top government officials claiming to have earned advanced degrees (including PhD's) really had not attended any schools of higher learning at all. Rather they had purchased degrees from an online diploma mill. Yet these individuals were being paid at those higher levels based on what was on their resumes.

Place Your Bets

What odds of success would you give a person blind, deaf, and without the ability to speak. Wait you say; a person who cannot see anything, cannot hear anything, and cannot formulate words as we know them? Yes, that's right. Well, most people would put the odds of success for this individual at less than zero. But one woman, at around the age of nineteen months old, developed a disease that robbed her of sight, sound, and the ability to speak; yet she went on to become a world renowned writer, putting the pen to some 12 published books.

Not only that, it is reported that she met with every President of the United States from President Grover Cleveland (President in the late 1800's) to President Lyndon Johnson (President in the mid 1960's). She befriended many famous people such as Mark Twain, Charlie Chaplin, and went on to become a world-renowned public speaker. No, most people would not have given Helen Keller even a small chance of accomplishing the many things she did with her life. Don't pick your winners too soon. How about this next one?

Taken Out Of School

He was taken out of school and separated from the other children when he was just a boy because the teacher said he was "slow." Today he might be labeled "special needs." But, he would go on to become one of the greatest inventors the world has ever known and earn the nickname "the Wizard of Menlo Park."

In what is considered one of the world's first R&D (research and development) laboratories, he and his team would generate more than a thousand patents in the 1800's; this would be incredible for anyone, even if it happened today.

For years, he and his team tried everything possible to discover a filament that would burn slowly and long enough in a vacuum; so that the light bulb could become a permanent fixture in modern society.

It is purported that he went through some 6,000 materials from the plant world alone in his search for the right filament; trying everything from strands of human hair, to platinum, fish line, even thread, but to no avail.

Then something extraordinary happened. He tried a piece of carbonated cardboard. The cardboard burned for over 300 hours, and thus the electric light bulb was born (in 1879) and forever changed the way people live their lives. By 1902, 18 million light bulbs were being used thanks to Thomas Edison (that boy that was labeled "slow" when he was in school). What if Thomas Edison had accepted the limits placed on him by others? He probably would not have had the success he eventually enjoyed. Don't pick your winners too soon.

My Own Experience

I can't stress to you enough times that declaring a person a superstar before the time can backfire on you and your organization. And ignoring other talent that is in your organization can cost your company millions. When I headed up a sales organization for a large Fortune 500 company, I watched all of the new salespeople come on board. Without fail, the majority of those who had the greatest resumes were not the top producers over the long haul. We called them a "flash in the pan." You see when they came on board they had all the right tools; an impressive resume, the ability to persuade others, and they dressed the part. They were great at formulating the right words to say to our clients, thus, they were able to fool people in the short run.

Success is a Marathon

Attaining success in any field is a marathon, not a sprint. The thing I had to constantly remind my leaders of was the fact that anyone can be a superstar for 90 days: but true winners are able to be top producers over long periods of time. What is the great equalizer? Hard work and determination. Give me a person willing to be coached, and willing to put in the necessary hours it takes to win any day, over a person who spends their time telling you how great they once was (by their resume). A resume tells you how well that person performed in the past, but does not tell you how well they will perform for your organization in the future.

Now, I'm not without knowledge in understanding we have to have a starting point for dialogue and conversations, but remember, the resume is not the "end all to beat all." Keep your eyes open for the next superstar and be willing to look at those who may not be on your "winner" radar. So, don't pick your winners too soon.

Leaders Recognize Talent

One of my greatest challenges and greatest joys in corporate America was leading a team of people. I was always reading, studying, and trying out new strategies on my team members. But the most fun I had each week was meeting with my leaders and listening to their knowledge. This may sound corny to you but I really felt privileged to be in their presence. Most of my leaders were much older than me, so I had the delicate task of leading them without coming across as a "know it all" or "the boss."

So what was the secret to my success? I had my team members talk most of the time. I engaged their minds and called on their years of experience. My part was to simply listen and learn. But the thing that shocked me every time we met was how much knowledge was in the room, and how much those leaders were willing to share. And you know what? The best ideas often came from the person most people would have over looked.

Leaders Get Input From Everyone

I knew I had some great talent on my team; so I didn't allow my leaders to just kick back and "watch" at the meetings. If they didn't participate, I'd help them feel a part of the group by asking something like this. "Hey, John; I noticed you haven't shared in this topic. What are your thoughts (opinions) on this matter? Believe me, everyone has an opinion- so my job was to get that person to share theirs with the group. Why? Because I never knew when an idea that seemed "dumb" to them, might be the answer I was looking for to a complex problem the team or organization was facing.

One of your jobs as a leader should be learning to recognize and engage the talent you have among you. Leaders recognize talent! Act like a talent scout and keep your eyes open at all times. Think of it this way: professional talent scouts make lots of money. Imagine being the talent scout who discovers a David Beckham, Michael Jordan, Kobe Bryant, Tiger Woods, Oprah, or a Justin Bieber. In fact, Simon Cowell, the former producer of American Idol has become a multi-millionaire with a show that spots talent. Even he has learned; don't pick your winners too soon.

People Are Your Greatest Asset

Another challenge you face as a leader today is learning how to seize the collective power of your greatest asset - people. Each person on your team brings to the table their own set of assets and liabilities. A key to leading a winning team of people is learning to play up their assets, while down playing their liabilities. I'll be the first to admit this is often easier said than done. But I can also report that it can be done - and done successfully. The point is to give everyone on your team a fair chance to showcase their talents.

It Starts Here

Your success starts with valuing people. You see, we respect what we value - and we value what we respect. Now, I want you to slow down and read this statement again: We respect what we value - and we value what we respect. Think for a moment, do you listen to people you don't respect? Let's say you know a person who never keeps their word. Every time you see them they offer you one excuse after another why they can't do what they have promised; and this has gone on for years. Would you listen to any new promises that person makes to you? Probably not. Well, if I won't listen to you - chances are I don't respect you. And if I don't respect you, I won't value your opinions or anything you say.

Valuing People Is Vital

Often when people are given something for free, they don't value it the same way as when they have saved their hard earned dollars to buy it. More often than not, a person who has saved for months, even years, to buy a car takes better care of that car than someone who was given a car. Now, I know there are exceptions to just about every rule; but this is true for most people. For this same reason it is said *"free advice is never worth the price people pay for it."* People pay nothing, so they think it's worth nothing.

But you know what? People are not as "dumb" as some suppose. They can tell if you value their opinion and are keenly aware when you do not. In this same vein, employees can tell when an organization values their opinions and when they do not.

You Deprive Yourself

When an organization fails to value employees' opinions they drastically limit their opportunity for discovering new strategies and new talent that can help them succeed. Imagine allowing a good employee to leave the organization prematurely and later discovering they had an idea for a product or service that could have caused the company's profits to soar. What the company did, in effect, was name their winners too soon; and the employee that left their organization too soon evidentially was not picked as one of the winners.

Valuing Requires Commitment

Authors Swanson and Holton writing in the *Human Resource Development Research Handbook* believed that in order to improve the performance of employees, organizations must value them and see them as assets. And then make a commitment to their long term effectiveness. When using the term development in human resource, subsequent terms such as: performance, productivity, learning, improvement, quality, efficiency, competency, outcomes, assessments, analysis, evaluation and value are basic nomenclature within the performance improvement milieu.

Authors Combs & Falletta concluded that in order to maintain a competitive advantage in today's global economy, organizations must continually search for opportunities to increase workplace performance and productivity (spot the talent among them). I know no better way to gain the competitive edge on your competition than to treat your people like they are your greatest assets (value them) and more importantly get this value message deep in their hearts and minds - We value your opinions.

Start A New Campaign

Start a new *"our people are our greatest asset"* campaign. This campaign should include training for leaders to educate them on talent management skills. This would include learning to appreciate the talent among them. The bottom line is everyone in the organization is given a fair chance at greatness. Give everyone a team uniform, put them on the field, and the cream will rise to the top, every time. However, be forewarned: the eventual leader of the pack just may surprise you.

One Final Bet

What odds would you give a child, born the last of ten children in the ghetto? With ten mouths to feed the family didn't have lots of money. Life from day to day was a struggle. In school, he was not particularly a standout in academics or sports. As a young child he was shy and reserved. In the school yearbook, he was not picked "most likely to succeed" at anything. In fact, you hardly noticed his picture. What odds would you place on him getting out of the ghetto and becoming a great success in life? A million to one? Well, most people placing a bet would take those odds; because the vast majority of people raised in the ghetto never get out. But let me remind you once more that there has never been a test devised that can determine who will and who won't succeed in life.

This man went on to become an honored military veteran, earned a PhD. in education, climbed the corporate ladder and lead a great team of people for twelve years, earned the top performance awards at every place he was employed, has written over 10 books and is a sought after professional speaker. Let me say one more time - don't pick your winners too soon!

What discoveries did you pick up from this chapter? Write your answers here:

1. ____

____

________________.

2. ____

____

_______________.

3. ____

____

_______________.

Now, when you add this next people principle to your arsenal for success and truly master it, you will automatically set yourself apart from the rest of the pack. So, don't stop now-let's keep going to Chapter 5...

Power Principle #4:

People Just Want A Fair Chance

CHAPTER FIVE

People Principle Number 5

People Will Rise to Your Level of Expectations

When you expect much you get much, when you expect little you get little.

-Cubie Davis King

Negative Words Cut Deep

A few months ago I was speaking to a group of business professionals in Arizona. It was a great audience and in my closing statements I challenged those leaders to lift the spirits of those they worked with and whose paths they crossed. I talked about how devastating negative words and comments are on people. And how leaders hold the key to making or breaking the teams of people they work with. "Negative words cut like a knife," I extolled, "and their wounds can last a lifetime." All of us can remember at least one incident from our childhood where mere words cut us deeply.

One Unbelievable Story

I had concluded my speech and was greeting people in the audience as they departed. Waiting in the back of the room was a gray haired gentleman, I'd say he was around sixty-five to seventy years old. He asked if he could share with me an incident that happened to him as a child. *Warning! This story will break your heart:* He told me when he was a child his father scolded him on a daily basis. It was like par for the course to get a daily dose of hate filled words thrown at him, he said. Everyday, he had to endure the torture of being told how dumb he was and how he'd never amount to anything in life. But on this one particular day, he said the words he heard from his dad scarred him for life.

He recalled the incident with vivid details as he told of how he came home with his 5th grade report card for his father to review and sign. After his father saw his grades, he was so disappointed at his performance that he exploded in anger and called him all sorts of unsavory names - names I dare not mention - even here.

It Still Hurts

Imagine for a second a young child (4 feet tall) being yelled at (by an adult 6 feet, 4 inches tall) and called names you wouldn't even call a dog. By this time, tears began to swell up in his eyes. It was all I could do to keep from crying myself. Here this man was in his late 60's to early 70's still literally feeling the pain of this horrific childhood incident as if it happened to him only yesterday.

After a few seconds he collected himself and continued. Then he told me that after he graduated from high school he was offered a full scholarship to become a military officer; but he turned it down because his father had convinced him (very early in his life) that he wasn't smart enough and that he would never amount to anything in life. He ended by saying he felt cheated out of all of life's possibilities. I thought of this man the rest of that evening, and think of him often today.

Leaders Have Great Responsibilities

As a leader, whether you're a boss, parent, teacher, or coach you bear a great responsibly to use all of your talents to help people win in life - not fail. The coach, Art Williams wrote:

> *"I see so many people in management today who are always cutting down their people. They'll go have a drink with a buddy and talk about how sorry their people are, how lazy they are, and how dumb they are."*

He went on to say, you must treat every person you hire as if they are going to be with you for life. Now, we all know employees come and go all the time, but for the time they are with you, if you want to get the best performance out of them, you've got to tell them that is what you expect, and then help them to achieve it.

Running people down does not create in them a desire to help you or the organization succeed. In fact, quite the contrary is more likely to happen. When people are treated badly, they often react badly. Yell at people and you are likely to get a negative response.

Think for a moment of this enormous responsibility you have been given - a chance to influence a life in a very meaningful way. And your influence on that person, whether for good or for bad, will last a lifetime.

Another Great Lesson

I often talk of the lessons I have learned in my nearly sixty years of life, and one of these lessons is this: *People rise to your level of expectations.* I have seen this played out in so many real life situations that I made it a point (with my wife) to instill high levels of expectations in our three children.

You see, I studied this particular people principle extensively for years and used it when I worked in corporate America, and when I volunteer my time with the Jr. Achievement Program teaching business courses to young people in middle schools, and at a non-profit organization where I volunteered to work with young people for some twenty years. I have personally tested this principal and used many people as samples in my studies.

Guess what? Without fail, I found this principle to be absolutely true. When I expected the best out of people - I got their best - not sometimes - but every time. Even when their best didn't come up to the standard I'd hoped for. What I learned from my experiments was when I told people that I expected their best, and (more importantly) that they were capable of reaching that top level, that people actually achieved what they thought was impossible. People really do rise to your level of expectations.

The Law of Attraction

The law of attraction has been studied for many decades. Napoleon Hill wrote about it in the early 1930's. In short the law of attraction says: We attract to ourselves that which we feel most worthy of. In other words we get what we expect.

If you wake up in the morning and declare that it's going to be a terrible day- guess what? You get exactly what you expect. If you expect you will dislike certain people, chances are no matter what they do, you're going to dislike them. Why? Because that's what you expect. If you expect that your team will sabotage your efforts, they will sabotage your efforts.

Expect the Best

Here's an idea- try just the opposite. Tell your people that they are the best (and then see them that way), and they will begin to perform their best. I witnessed this many times when I lead a team of sales professionals. I told them they were the best in class, and proved to them I meant every word (even when we didn't meet our monthly goals). I kept right on telling them they were the best. After a while they started believing it themselves.

The Mirror Strategy

Remember I told you earlier about the case Napoleon Hill talked about where this one company during the great depression, put mirrors on the backs of each sales truck and instructed their salespersons that they were not to call on any prospects until they could look in that mirror and first convince themselves they could make the sale. When companies all around them were failing, this one company prospered. What happened? Those sales people began to expect the best.

Taking a page right out of his book, I had mirrors installed in my offices, and wrote on the mirrors (with a dry eraser marker) different messages for each week. I wrote things like "I'm a top gun;" "today I will win;" and "I'm the best in the west" (our offices were in California). So, every time our salespeople looked in the mirror to fix their clothes, these subliminal messages appeared above their heads. It wasn't long before they actually started believing those messages and our team really did become tops in the company.

Go into the locker rooms of any winning teams and you'll see these types of subliminal messages posted throughout those spaces. Let me tell you of another experience of how people rise to your level of expectations.

Statistics Made Easy

When I was in college working toward my bachelor's degree in business, I had to take a mandatory business statistics class which included calculus. Not only did I struggle, but about 70% of the entire class was struggling. But we had a professor who had developed an innate ability to motivate a team of people. Evidently he understood that people rise to your level of expectations.

One day, sensing that the entire class was just not "getting it," he told everyone to close their books. After we closed our books, he told us to close our eyes and repeat these words after him, "statistics is easy," he said. So we repeated after him, "statistics is easy." "This is fun," so we repeated "this is fun." "I get it now," he said, and we repeated, "I get it now." While we had our eyes closed he told us to picture ourselves as actually doing the problems and getting them correct. This went on for about ten minutes. The he told us to take a fifteen minute break.

Our Amazing Transformation

When the class reconvened, it was like magic. For me and the entire class a light bulb seemed to have gone off in our heads. From that very day, I really began to have fun, the work became much easier, and I couldn't wait to get to class from that day on. Talking to my fellow classmates they said they felt the same. For the first time I "got" statistics. But more importantly, it affirmed once again that people rise to your level of expectations. The professors could have called us a bunch of dummies and given up on us but, he made a lasting impact on my mind. An impact I feel is now my duty to pass on to others.

Leaders Can Change People

As a leader you can make people believe, even when it looks impossible. One of the easiest things to do is to put people down. You don't need a high IQ to accomplish this. But those leaders who make a positive and lasting impact on people's lives are the ones who know how to build other people's self esteem.

Take the Bitter with the Sweet

Most people love others as long as things are good; but what about when things goes bad? True leaders will stick with the team. When a sports team makes all the way to the playoffs, even the finals, and then falls short of the championship, it is devastating. But the coach doesn't throw the baby out with the bath water. True leaders stay and rebuild, and with perseverance and "pit bull" tenacity they fight their way to a championship.

You must stay with your people when it's good and when it's bad, when it's bitter and when it's sweet. So they didn't meet the projections for the quarter; help your people rebuild and they will return the favor with a dedication to their work that will amaze you. I will admit; it takes a special leader who has developed special people skills to pull this off. But these are people skills anyone can learn - including you.

Would You Fire Yourself

Make an honest assessment of how you treat people. If the shoe was on the other foot, and you were on the other end of the way you talk to and treat other people, would you fire yourself?

Would you invite the other you to hang out with other employees? When the other you walks in the break room, would you get up and walk out? What would you say about the other you behind your back? Would it be true? I want you to ponder these questions and get your people to ponder these questions.

He Came Close to Firing Himself

The people skills of Andrew Carnegie are legendary. I highly recommend everyone to study this man. The story is told of how Mr. Carnegie took a liking to a young man in his company. He believed the young man was brilliant and was planning to invite him to become a part of his mastermind group. The mastermind group was a small elite group of professionals handpicked by Mr. Carnegie to work directly with him in building and running his company.

When the young man found out he was to be inducted into this elite group, he began to celebrate, howbeit too soon. He began to drink heavily and run around with people he once shunned. His performance at work began to slip when he began showing up to work hung over day after day.

After letting this go on for about three months, Mr. Carnegie invited the young man to talk over dinner. After a full course meal they retired to his study. Mr. Carnegie told the young man to sit in his chair. After he was seated he said, "now you are the boss and I am you - what would you do to me if I was acting like you?"

Ashamed, the young man said, "Mr. Carnegie I know you're going to fire me so please don't prolong it. Let's get it over with." Mr. Carnegie said, "no; I'm not going to fire you - if I was going to fire you, I would not have fed you that good meal; I could have done that at the office." "I just wanted to know what would you do?" The young man reportedly said that he'd fire himself. But Andrew Carnegie would not let him do it.

Great Leaders Know How to Redeem

Leaders with strong people skills know how to bring out the best in their people. It's not hard to kick a person when they are down, any coward can do that. But it takes a person who knows who they are, and with supreme confidence in their own abilities, to help a person back up.

Well, as the story goes, that young man became a star pupil of Mr. Carnegie and went on to become a multi-millionaire.

Lessons Learned

Did this chapter have a positive impact on your thinking? How so? List three things you learned from this chapter:

1. ____
____
________________.

2. ____
____
________________.

3. ____
____
________________.

Now, this next people principle truly holds the key to your success. Not only is it powerful, but when it is done right, it is actually fun. But don't be fooled by the fun part, it is highly effective when dealing with other people. Let the excitement continue right into Chapter 6 – Wow this one is good! Let's read it now…

People Principal #5:

People Will Rise
To Your Level Of Expectations

CHAPTER SIX

People Principle Number 6

People Want You to Recognize Their Contributions

Show people your heartfelt thanks for an outstanding effort, and they are most likely to respond again with an outstanding effort.

-Cubie Davis King

People Are Starving

There is one thing every person in every organization wants more than anything other thing. In fact, studies after studies have proven they want this much more than even money itself. Everyday when they come to work, they look for it in one way or another. In fact, they want it so bad they are literally starving for it. Yet many organizations still don't get it. The funny part about it is - it doesn't have to be big or expensive. Even small displays of appreciation can have a major impact on a person's daily performance.

So what is this thing people are starving for? People crave praise and recognition. You see, innate in every person on this earth, regardless of race, color, creed, culture, or religion is this deep desire to be recognized. To be held in high esteem for a job well done. To be "the example" of the person that gets things done. It's inside every one of us. And though it may get muted over time, I believe it never ever goes away; it remains a part of us throughout our entire lives.

Some People Don't Get It

A few years ago, while consulting with a marketing company, I was invited to sit in on one of their call center's weekly meetings, and then provide feedback to leadership on how the process could be improved. The turnover rate in that department was horrendous at about 70%. Obviously there was something very wrong. As the employees gathered in the training room I couldn't help but notice their lack of enthusiasm. They literally dragged in one after another, shoulders drooped and wearing no smiles. The place was dead silent as they waited for their "boss." I knew things were bad just by watching their demeanor; but I was about to find out first hand, just how bad things really were.

Enter the Intimidator

Walking in a few minutes later was the person who headed up the department - "the boss". He was a menacing figure who never smiled, and walked as if he was wearing two six shooters around his waist. He appeared to take great pride in the fact that the employees were frightened of him. Then he began to talk.

What I heard caused my mouth to drop open. And that is saying a lot coming from a nine year military veteran who survived everything from yelling drill sergeants in boot camp, to nasty company commanders. In a word, I was shocked! The guy started screaming (not talking but screaming) at the employees as he pranced back and forward in front of the room, like a lion protecting her cubs. He used enough obscenities to make a drunken sailor blush, as he went around the room calling employees by names and threatening to fire them if they didn't improve their sales numbers. The whole thing so sickened me, that I refused to look at the guy after the first five minutes; it was that bad.

Failure Leaves Clues

What this so called "boss" did to those employees was absolutely criminal. And I guarantee none of them will ever forget the way he made them feel (remember Chapter 1). I guess my disgust could not be hidden (and believe me I tried), because, the next day I was summoned to his office. He told me I disrespected him by not showing enthusiasm for his techniques; because "employees were looking at the way I was reacting." I knew then (because of his nasty techniques) that I couldn't continue on that contract so I immediately tendered my resignation from that assignment, and was more than ecstatic to return all of their money. I didn't want my name remotely associated with anything that beat up on people in that fashion.

Predictable Failure

Well, needless to say that business went bust. Are you surprised? I wasn't. Just like success leaves clues, failure does too. No business can survive long range with a turnover rate of 70%. This business spent the bulk of their profits recruiting and training new people. Even a senior in high school doing this math would know it wouldn't add up. Here is another discovery I made as a result of consulting with hundreds of organizations around the county:

> *"Companies spend billions of dollars every year on the latest technology, then hire people who literally chase good employees away."*

Now, Back To the Good Stuff

Just reading about that guy was a downer wasn't it? So let's get back to how to get the most out of your team by using praise and recognition. Like children, adults need to be encouraged. Even those who are self motivated must have some positive input from others from time to time.

I said earlier that praise and recognition are more desirable than money. That recognition can come in the form of a degree, or it can be as simple as a plaque to hang on the wall. When you see a team win the championship in their particular sport, do they hold up a bucket of money? No, they hoist the trophy. When golfers wins a major tournament, do they roll out a wheelbarrow full of money? No, they present a trophy or green jacket. You see, long after the money is gone, and their bodies can't play that sport any longer, they will remember that feeling they got when they were *recognized as being the best.*

Now, I'm not without knowledge. Sure they get paid; because that is what they do for a living. But ask any former professional ball player about their career and few will say their greatest moments were when they made a zillion dollars. No, they will say it was when they made the winning touchdown, scored that winning basket, or hit that improbable shot on the 18th Green to win the Masters.

Few Ever Know

Did you know that few people working in organizations today have ever had the satisfaction of knowing just how good it feels to win and be recognized for doing something great? Prior to joining the U.S. Navy, I had never received an award of any kind as an adult. When I say award, I mean being held in high esteem and brought before a company of my peers and presented an award. Never in my adult life had that happened.

I want you to keep this one thing in mind as I walk you through how this can have a profound effect on the people in your organization and spurring them on to do great things for your company. Then I'll show you how easy it is to implement a rewards and recognition program. This first thing to remember here is this: most adults have never had the experience those professional ball players have had. That experience of being recognized in front of a company of their peers for doing something spectacular for the team.

Good Behavior is Addictive Also

We know that bad behavior has a negative impact on people's lives; but the reverse is also true. You can also incite and inspire good habits in other people by using the same tactic people use for bad habits. For example on the bad side: if you reward a person in the organization in spite of the fact that they are always late for work and for company meetings, what message are you sending to your other employees? "Hey, you can break the company policies and still be a superstar."

Conversely, when you reward good behavior and hold those individuals up as superstars, the message is clear: if you want the same treatment, do the same things. The winner inside of the people, who crave this type of recognition, (this good behavior) rises up and says; "hey me too. I want to be a part of something special also." Again, most working adults have never had this incredible experience.

My Very First Award

Graduating high school and departing immediately for the military was the right choice for me. I was young and inexperienced, but bright eyed and bushy tailed. The one thing my father taught me from a child, was to be a sharp dresser. Since clothes cover almost 80% of our bodies, he knew the power of first impressions, from being a military man himself (my father was a World War II veteran).

While attending my first military training school (I was 18 years old at the time), the command conducted these random locker inspections to see how well we kept our living quarters; there was never a clue as to when the Captain would visit your space. Well, I kept my clothes locker organized in the exact same way we were taught in boot camp. To me, it made good sense, because it allowed me to get to my things quickly and easily.

On the weekends, I'd spend my Sundays ironing my uniforms and getting organized for the entire week. That way, I didn't have to worry about if they were up to par, and this system freed me to get directly to my homework each night (we had lots of homework). So it was the perfect system for me.

Surprise, Surprise, Surprise

Then early one Monday morning, without warning, we were told to stand down and stand in front of our lockers. While we stood at attention, the Commander inspected each person's bunk and locker individually. When he got to my locker, he stopped abruptly. He looked at me and then looked at my locker. He looked at me again and then looked at my locker again. "Do you always keep your locker this way,' he asked. "Yes sir," I replied. My heart was racing while trying to figure out what I had done wrong. You see, he didn't ask anyone else that question; so I thought I had to be doing something wrong. "Take down his name and rank," he said, to his assistant. Then he ordered everyone to "carry on" as he walked out the door. And that is the way he left it that day. I thought to myself, "wow you must be in real trouble now." Days went by without a single word.

Be the Example

Then once again, without warning he showed up in my classroom. His assistant called everyone to attention. "Seaman King, front and center" was the command. It seemed like forever as I marched up in front of the class (while my heart seemed to beat right out of my chest). What did I do wrong, I wondered? Could it have been that bad? Why wasn't anyone else cited for whatever I did? I just couldn't understand why this was happening.

Then I got the surprise of my life. The Commander began to read from a citation awarding me the distinction of being the most "squared away" (best dressed and most organized) sailor on the entire base. I was completed blown away. I was just doing me (as my sister, Jerrelyn says) - or just being myself. It was one of the proudest moments of my life. You might ask why this award would mean so much to me. Well, this award was special for two reasons: (1) Remember, I said, my dad instilled in me at an early age to dress for success? This award was a testament to my dad's solid teaching, and (2) prior to that, I had never received an award in my adult life. I became the example for all to see and it felt good.

The Powerful Aftermath

The impact of that award went far beyond me. Looking back on that occasion, it is apparent to me now that the Commander knew exactly what he was doing. And because he made the award with great fanfare, it set off a firestorm of copycats wanting to be recognized for being a "top gun." From that day on, many of my shipmates began to follow in my footsteps; many of them asked me to share my ideas with them on how to iron their uniforms and organize their lockers. I was asked many details, even down to the cologne I wore. Well, I was proud to share my secrets with them.

What They Really Wanted

But I want you to think for a moment. What were my shipmates really craving? The same things people crave in organizations around the world - praise and recognition. And they want to be praised and recognized in the company of their peers. It is a fact; good behavior can also be duplicated in your organization. What powerful principals do you suppose was at work there? Write your answers here:

____

____

____

____

____

____.

Reinforcers

At that time, in all my 18 years on the earth, I had never known such a feeling - that feeling of standing in front of my peers, and being recognized as one of the best. It felt great! So great - that I wanted more of it. Well, I went on to receive top awards at every place I've worked at (now spanning over some 37 years), and now I teach these principles (how to be a top performer, and get the best performance out of your teams) to companies and organizations the world over.

Often referred to as the father of the behavior science, B.F. Skinner advanced the science from speculative mathematical suppositions, to hardcore measurements of observed intelligence. He investigated, analyzed, and evaluated behavior. In his groundbreaking work, *About Behaviorism,* Skinner explored the powerful question "how can another person be induced to behave in a given way." His answer: reinforcers (better know as incentives). He concluded that when a behavior is followed by a certain kind of consequence, it is more likely to occur again. In short, if you want good performance to be repeated time and again by your people, use praise and recognition.

Great Leaders Have Always Known

Study the history of the most successful organizations in history and you'll find leaders who understood the power of what I call praise reinforcement. How does praise reinforcement work? First, praise the performer for good behavior! Then, you reinforce it – praise the performer, then reinforce! What this does is train the minds of your team to believe they can achieve great things. Even when it seems like they are losing, keep praising and providing incentives for good behavior.

One of the best ways to accomplish this is to always recognize at least 20% of your people at every meeting you have. Let's say you have 20 team members at a meeting; pick at least 4 people that are doing an outstanding job and call them up to be recognized. This seemingly small, inconsequential gesture - when done correctly - can have a profound, positive effect on the rest of the team. Toward the end of this chapter, I'll show you exactly how to do this, and be successful doing it every time.

Lesson of Vince Lombardi

By all accounts, this famed football coach was tough as nails. But he knew how to use praise and recognition to perfection. I remember seeing him as a child when the Green Bay Packers would play my home team, the Dallas Cowboys, in the Cotton Bowl, in Dallas (in the early 1960's). By halftime Dallas Cowboys fans had already started leaving because the Packers were beating Dallas like a drum. But, I always found Vince Lombardi fascinating.

If there is one thing Vince Lombardi stood for, it was excellence. He believed in it wholeheartedly. And his weapon of choice in motivating other people was faith. He made people believe they were much better than they thought they were - and they returned the favor - by performing better than they thought they could. Do you get the connection?

He Built a Dynasty with People

W. Clement Stone was another person who ascended to the highest levels of society by mastering the art of successfully dealing with people. Born poor, by the age of 6 he was selling newspapers on the streets of Chicago (South Side). There, he began perfecting his people skills. His polite charm won people over time and again. Having developed and perfected impeccable people skills, he went on to build the Combined Insurance Company of America, and in 11 short years (by 1930) he had over a thousand agents selling insurance for him. Unprecedented for that day and time. In 2008, the company he started sold for nearly $3 billion dollars.

In the powerful book he co-authored with Napoleon Hill, *Success Through a Positive Mental Attitude,* he wrote:

"You can motivate others by having faith in them. Faith, rightly understood, is active not passive. Active faith...risks failure because it assumes it will succeed. When you have that type of faith in another person, they will succeed." This is the exact same conclusion coach Vince Lombardi came to. There is something very powerful in this philosophy.

People Want To Win

It's my firm belief that people want to do a good job for their organizations. But just like a child in grade school, they need to be motivated. Effective motivation turns the focus from a "me boss-you worker" mentality, to a "what can I do to help you succeed" mentality. What's that saying? "Help enough people get what they want, and you'll automatically get what you want." Effective leaders know how to share the spot light with their people – because, in the end who gets the ultimate recognition for getting the job done - The leader!

It takes absolutely nothing from you to put your people on a pedestal and say, "you did a great job." Quite the contrary, your people will see you in a different light and will return the favor with a new dedication to their work.

You may say, that sounds rosy to me. "Believe me, I've worked for two of the largest corporations in the Fortune 500, served in the military, and worked in the federal government.

This gave me firsthand knowledge and years of experience working in some tough dog-eat-dog - can you swim with the sharks?" workplaces. Not only did I survive but I thrived and won. These people principles will work, if you work them.

A Bad System is a Bad System

In the field of Human Performance Improvement (HPI) the work of the performance technologist is to help an organization improve their human systems (help their people succeed). As I mentioned earlier, people are your organization's greatest assets, and they must be valued as such. Gary Rummler, considered to be one of the forerunners in the field of Human Performance Improvement (HPI) said this:

Take a good person and pit them against a bad system, And the system will win every time!"

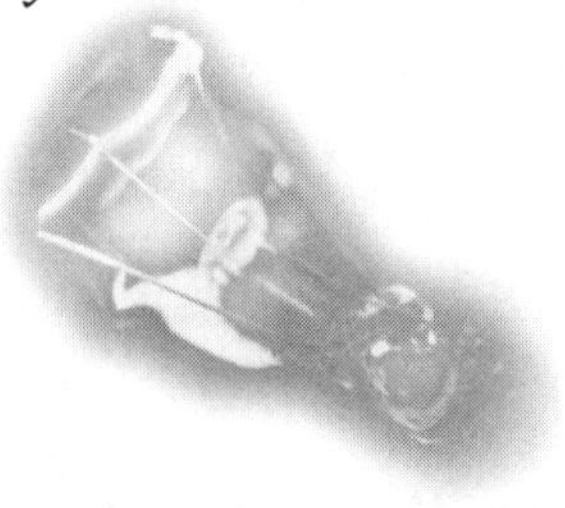

As a leader, you can make all the difference as to whether an employee succeeds or fails. Think of it this way: you have a chance to make a real difference in the lives of other people. Of course you have to have a willing subject - but given their attention- do not let them down. As a leader, manager, supervisor, parent, teacher, etc. it is in your hands - so do good by them.

Strategies for Success

Now I want to share with you some of the strategies and techniques I used to take my team to the national championship (if you will) in our company. These techniques helped (what most people would call) ordinary people to do extra ordinary things.

First Things First

Step 1 – Get Excited: The very first thing you must understand in putting together an awesome awards and recognition program for your organization is that it must be exciting; and those running the program must be excited. Imagine a person putting their hand on a hot iron and simply walking away without showing any emotions whatsoever. If there is life in their body, there will be some excitement there. They may run, scream, dance, or what have you, but there will be some type of emotions displayed. So there has to be some excitement for this whole thing to work.

Remember the story I told of being brought before my entire military class and presented an award? Even in the military there was excitement - and the results were measurable. So I have two words for you as you set up your rewards and recognition program - **GET EXCITED!** And remember, to recognize at least 20% of your people (praise them) at every meeting you have. Hold them up as examples of those who are doing a great job for the organization.

Step 2 – Invest in TYC:

Invest in a stack of thank you cards. Go to an office supply store and buy a lot of these cards. This is one of the most effective tools in your recognition toolbox. It's amazing to me, have much good will you will spread when you use these simple cards- especially today in this email, voicemail, texting, and instant messaging society.

Think about this: When is the last time you got a hand written thank you note from anyone? And even if you have, there are not many. This is what makes sending thank you cards so special to the people you send them to; a teacher, a client, or an employee. I made it a point that when a person did a great job to leave a thank you note in my own handwriting, with a small token of appreciation like a small piece of chocolate, or a gift card for a cup of coffee. The note would say something like this:

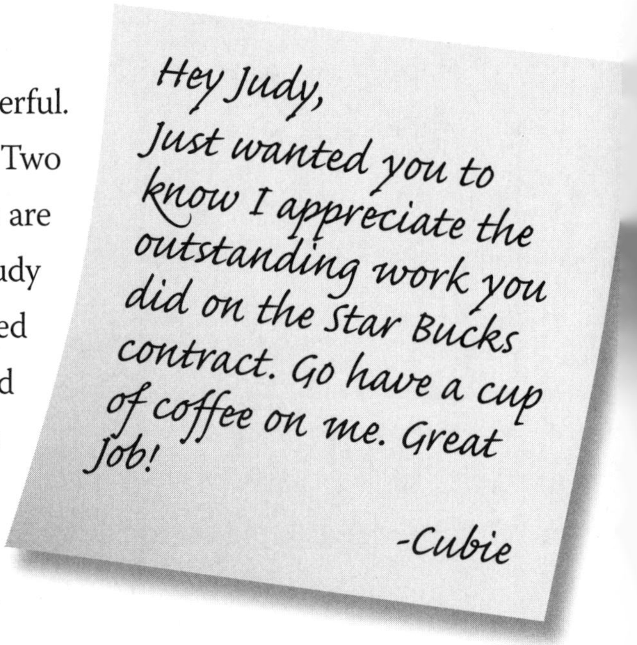

Simple - but powerful. Why is this so powerful? Two very powerful dynamics are at work here. First, Judy knows I've recognized her contributions, and that I appreciate her as well. And second, Judy gets that feeling that I thought enough of her and her work to take time out of my busy schedule to handwrite a special thank you note to her.

Now, what's the benefit for me? I've now built some good will with Judy. Let's say we are in a work crunch and need to get some reports to corporate and it will require staying late. I'm willing to bet Judy will help me out in that crunch.

When you praise and recognize people, it has to be genuine. Remember, people can smell a phony a mile away. This has to come from your heart. So, what if people don't help me out in the future? I'll still recognize them for a job well done. At some point they will get the message that you really do care. So make good use of thank you cards! Be copious with your praise.

Step 3 – Keep Small Gifts in Your Desk

I'm going to let you in on one of my best kept secrets for motivating people. Here it is: you don't have to spend a lot of money to get a lot of mileage out of your recognition program. In fact, you're going to be surprised how little you'll need to invest. Remember, we said that money is a poor motivator when it comes to getting better performance out of your employees. So here is a list of some of the gifts I gave out to employees.

Keep in mind it was not the gift itself that got them excited, it was the recognition, how it was conducted, and ultimately how it made the employee feel. I'll tell you exactly how I gifted the awards coming up next. For now here is a list of some of the gifts I kept on hand.

Gift: Pack of Extra Chewing Gum

Cost: Less than $2.00

Award Name: "The Extra Award" given to those employees who gave a little extra effort for the week.

Gift: M&M's Candy (plain & peanut)

Cost: Less than $5.00

Award Name: "The More & More Award" given to the employee I could count on to do more and more (hence M&M).

Gift: 100 GRAND Candy Bar

Cost: Less than $2.00

Award Name: "The 100 Grand Award" given to salespeople who sold at least $100,000 in products for the quarter.

Gift: Crunch Candy Bar

Cost: Less than $2.00

Award Name: "The Crunch Award" given to those employees who gave their best efforts during the end of the month crunch time.

Others Awards Included:

Plaques

Trophies

Movie Tickets

Gift Cards (all sorts for dinner, shopping, music downloads)

Flowers

Tickets to ball games

Oil changes

Discount Coupons

And just about anything else

Have Some Fun

To say that I had fun with my recognition and awards program is an understatement. I had a blast! The reason I got so excited was every time I gave out an award, I saw the look of appreciation on that person's face, and it took me back to the time when I received that first award (in the military). I saw in the eyes of adults, people who had never, ever, been appreciated like that in their lives.

Step 4 – The Award Presentation

To add that extra touch - I kept an instant Polaroid camera (the kind that printed the picture on the spot), and I had one of my managers take a picture for our "wall of fame" where we would post them. And like children showing off their best coloring project at open house - adults would walk up to that wall and stare at their picture. It was especially touching when a family member came to visit them. I wondered sometimes if they invited their family to come by the office, just so they could show off their pictures? If they did, it was alright with me. I felt proud watching them being proud.

That program was so effective, I see people that worked with me back then, now some 23+ years later, and they talk of those days as if it were yesterday. Talk about having an impact. People never forget the way you make them feel!

Be Creative with Your Program

Anything and everything can be used as an award. I'd walk down the aisles of stores and ideas would literally pop in my head; because one of the advantages, I had, was I got to know the people I worked with and got to know some of their likes and dislikes. Folks; get genuinely interested in your people!

Another Creative Area

Another creative area you can capitalize on is finding out what employees' children like. No; you don't have to ask them. Go back and review People Principle Number 3? That's all you have to do. I can tell you this: If you want to win my heart over, be kind to my children. And I'm no different than every other parent in this world.

Let's say I'd have an employee with a child in college (they told me this – I didn't have to ask); I'd listened to find out what school their child was attending, and when they would do a good job I'd do something for their child. One of the things I did was award Starbuck's gift cards. College age adults like to hang-out around coffee houses; which brings me to this next point in the recognition system.

Step 5 – The Award Ceremonies

I gave awards out at weekly meetings, monthly meetings, quarterly meetings, and at our annual conventions. As I mentioned, you can award:Gift coupons for Starbucks, Wal-Mart, local restaurants, movies, gas cards, the Apple Store, iTunes, game rentals, local golf courses, sports tickets, flowers, etc. Plaques of all types from wooden to glass. Even trips to exotic places (for top guns only). The point is you are limited only by your own imagination. Wow, just talking about how much fun I had takes me back to those incredible days.

Of course the more people I had attend the ceremony, and the bigger the event, the more elaborate the awards were. How many people are we to recognize at any given meeting? At the very least 20 per cent. Don't worry, because at the 20% level, no one will feel you are overdoing it.

At my weekly and monthly meetings I'd end the meeting by calling the person(s) up front and making the award(s). At my quarterly meeting I'd reverse it and start the meeting off with the awards. And at our annual conventions I'd take an entire evening and do nothing but awards. But one important difference was to have the employee invite a member of their family to accompany them on stage.

All Hands on Deck

During all of the awards presentations I'd always have some of my managers stand and form a line and when the employee is called up, they were to high five them down the aisle as I played some upbeat music. It was electrifying and people actually looked forward to those award ceremonies.

Try It for Yourself

For those of you who have never experienced excitement like this in an organization, I can understand your skepticism. The first time I attended such a ceremony, I could not believe it was a Fortune 500 company. Take a look at any organization that is tops in their field and I'd guarantee you there is excitement that emanates from the very top. It's hard not to get excited if your house is on fire! PRAISE and RECONITION - when done properly, will increase employee productivity and boost your organization all the way to the top.

Lessons Learned

List three strategies you can employ in creating or expanding your employee recognition and awards program. Write your answers here:

1. ____

____

____.

2. ____

____

____.

3. ____

____

____.

If you don't employ this final principle, nothing in this book will mean anything to the people you encounter in your life. It is the chief cornerstone when dealing with other people. In Chapter 7 you'll discover just how important this principle really is. Quick, let's go there now...

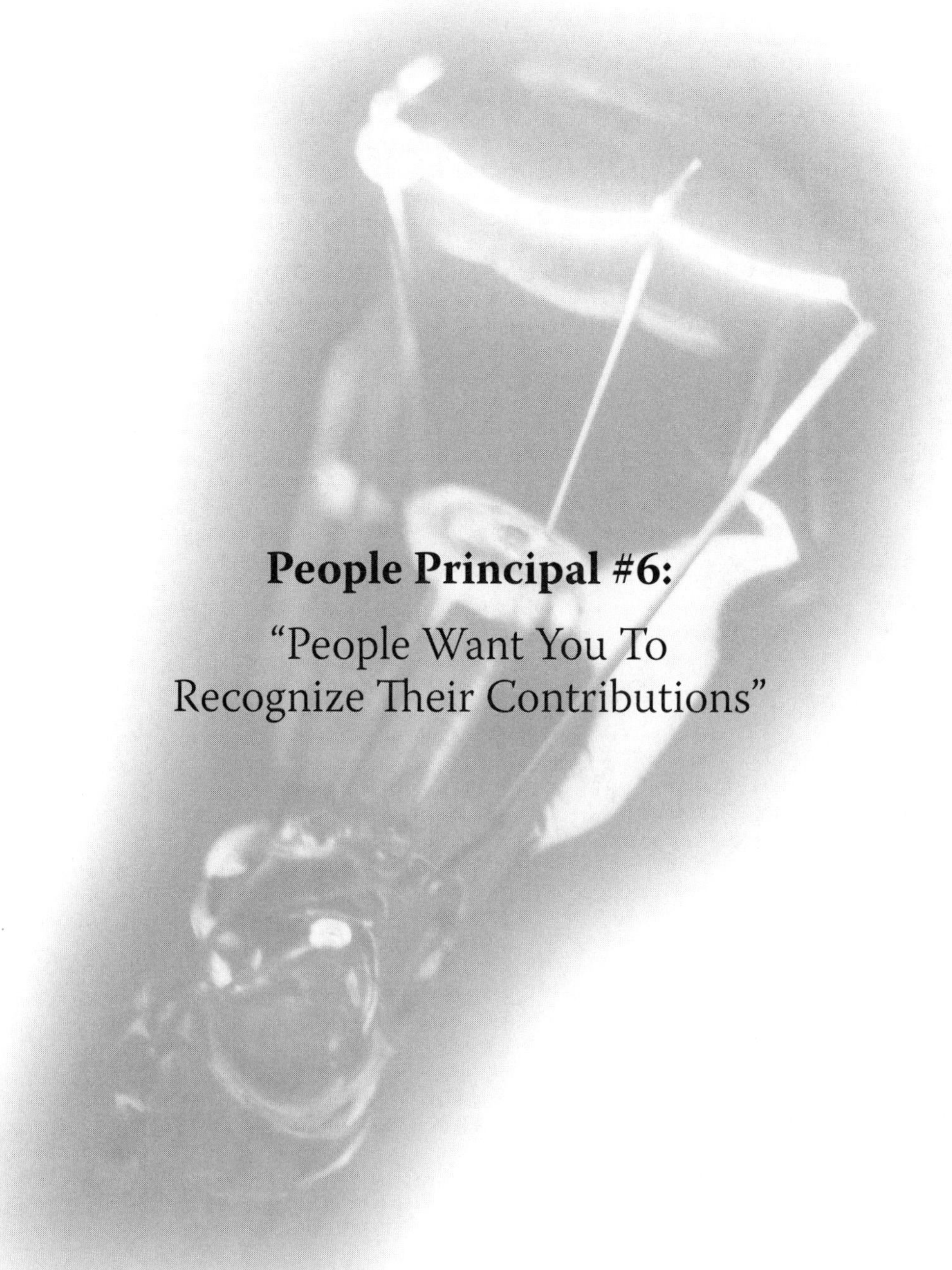

People Principal #6:

"People Want You To Recognize Their Contributions"

CHAPTER SEVEN

People Principle Number 7

People Want You to Do What You Promise

"The fastest and easiest way to discourage and demoralize people in an organization is to tell them one thing, and then do another"

-Cubie Davis King

A Person's Word Used To Be Bond

Ted was a promising new sales representative with an upstart financial services company. He came in earlier and stayed later than all of the other salespeople. He paid close attention to details and went the extra mile with all of his clients, making sure they understood the products and services they were investing in. He was an astute, savvy, and well-read individual who had all the makings of a superstar. Ted was excited about his work and exciting to watch; and nothing excites a sales organization like excitement.

Then it Happened!

One day, Ted was summoned to the office of the regional manager. When he arrived, he was taken to lunch and given the royal treatment. Afterwards, he was invited back to the office to sit down with the regional manager to discuss his future with the company. "Ted my boy," he said, "you have a very bright future with this company." "From all indications you will be the next district manager in our northern region." "Really," came the reply, "what do I have to do," asked Ted. "You just keep putting up the numbers you're putting up now for the next six months and you are assured that position," the regional manager said, as he patted Ted on the shoulder, and walked him to the door.

Ted left that office that day on cloud nine; and for the next six months he worked like a mad man, even doubling his sales numbers over that six months period. Occasionally, the regional manager would call or text him, telling him he was watching the numbers and things were on track.

However, during the last month (of this six month period), the calls and texts stop coming. Thinking the regional manager was just busy; Ted ignored the warning signs that something may be wrong. So, during the last week of that six month period, Ted decided to pick up the phone and call the regional manager's office.

Much to his surprise and dismay he found out that the regional manager had abruptly quit the job and had moved on.

Ted was devastated. How could a person do this to another human being, he thought? The regional manager had used Ted as a springboard and stepping stone for his own selfish purposes; disregarding Ted's feelings. What a shame; because there was a time when a person's word alone was their bond (or assurance) that what they promised you, they would honor.

People Rely on You

As a leader, your people rely on you to make good on your promises. Now let me make one thing clear; I know that life happens and things sometimes just don't work out the way we plan. That is different. What I'm talking about is leaders making promises with absolutely no intentions whatsoever of fulfilling those promises.

The Three Strikes Rule

I have what I call the three strikes rule and it goes like this:

- **Strike One:** If a leader makes a promise and breaks that promise the first time there is automatic forgiveness; things happen, and I don't want to be so callous that I won't take this into consideration. However, at some point I would hope that person would explain what happened and why they were not able to keep their promise.
- **Strike Two:** If the same person makes the same or another promise and breaks that promise, then that

raises an eye brow and I proceed with extreme caution. They might make good on the promise, or they might not. At this point I'm still willing to let them explain why they were unable to fulfill their promise.

- **Strike Three:** If that same leader makes the same or another promise and breaks that promise - my rule is run don't walk from that individual. These types of people can cause you to lose big, especially in business. The trust factor between the two parties has now been broken; and trust is a very fragile thing. When it is breached in this manner, it is hard to repair that breach.

Who Can Forget Enron?

If you want to further study the negative impact that broken promises have on people in an organization, the now defunct energy company ENRON is the perfect test tube case. What happened there brought dishonesty and broken promises to employees to a new low.

Formed in 1985, Enron was once was a shining star high on top of a hill, where everyone could see it. At its height, the company earned a whopping $100 billion in revenue in the year 2000 alone. But something sinister was brewing underneath that public facade. The company and its accounting agency, Arthur Andersen was hiding the fact that the company was cooking the books and padding the numbers it was reporting to its shareholders. The company hid billions of dollars in debts from deals that fell apart through elaborate accounting schemes created by senior leaders.

The Company Was Sinking

The sad part is, the leaders at Enron knew the company was sinking. Enron's stock went from a high of $90 dollars in early 2000 (their banner year), to less than $1 by November 2001. Shocking was the revelation that while the company's stock was sinking, the leaders at Enron were actively encouraging employees to buy more shares on their promises that the price of the shares would soon rebound.

What employees didn't know was at the same time they were being told to buy more shares; those same leaders were actively and aggressively unloading their stock. Talk about the ultimate betrayal. Those same leaders also (1) misled Enron's board of directors, (2) misled the auditing branch of the company; and (3) all but threatened Arthur Andersen to keep quiet about what was going on.

By December 2001, Enron filed for Chapter 11 bankruptcy, and with it, caused the collapse of one of the five largest accounting firms in the world - Arthur Andersen. Enron Employees and shareholders lost almost $11 billion. Enron leaders looked those employees in the eyes and promised them everything would be just fine, while they lined their pockets with millions.

Employees Were Devastated

I will never forget the images I saw on television where Enron's employees were left to virtually fend for themselves; as one after another, walked out of those beautiful offices in Houston, Texas, for the last time, with all of their belongings in boxes. I watched interview after interview of disillusioned and demoralized employees telling how they had lost everything, including their pensions, which they had earned over many years of service. How did this happen? Honest people, relying on dishonest people, who, from the start, never intended to keep their promises. Take another look at the quote that I wrote underneath this Chapter title, it says:

The fastest and easiest way to discourage and demoralize people in an organization is to tell them one thing, and then do another

We have seen similar scenarios like Enron played out in businesses, religious organizations, schools, non-profits, for profits, laws enforcement, governments, etc, etc; promises made and promises broken.

Lessons Learned

What lessons can you extrapolate from what the employees experienced at Enron? Write your answers here:

Let me emphasize once again that I'm not talking about not being able to keep a promise made in good faith- things do happen. When this happens, great leaders try their very best to rectify the situation as soon as possible. What I'm referring to here are leaders who have no intention of ever fulfilling the promises they have made to their people. And you know what? People may not ever say it, but when this happens, they lose all respect for those individuals.

What is Your Brand?

Whether you realize it or not, you (through your actions) have branded yourself. And everyday you are setting an example for other people to follow, whether it's a good example or a bad example. Imagine yourself having a large whiteboard strapped on the front and back of you (covering you from your neck to your feet), with a written message that other people can clearly see and read. This board is attached to you twenty-four hours a day, seven days a week, and for 365 days out of the year.

Try as you may, but you can't detach this board. What is this board? It is the 'who I am " billboard; and every person walking this earth gets one for life.

Now, on your board is a daily advertisement, just like a commercial on television, radio, or YouTube. And the funny part is you can't stop these daily broadcasts, they go out whether you like it or not. From the moment you wake in the morning, and throughout the day, regardless of what uniform you are wearing (whether it's a suit, a football uniform, or a nursing, police, firemen, or military uniform). You can be a CEO, doctor, lawyer, or even a teacher, but this one thing is true; you are setting an example for others to follow, whether it's a good example or a bad example. And each and everyday the people who cross your path recognized your brand.

Some people have established a brand of always being late to meetings. Others advertise themselves as being chronic complainers. Still others have a reputation for not keeping their promises. Every time you interact with other people, whether it's verbal or non-verbal, you advertise your brand. Here are some of the other brands people advertise on a daily basis (see Figure 3):

- I am difficult to get along with.
- I break my promises.
- I like to make people feel rotten.
- I'm the boss and what I say goes; regardless.

- No one is more important than me.
- Do as I say, not as I do.
- I'm always late for everything.
- I hear you talking but I'm not listening.

Figure 3. Examples of some "who I am " branding messages.

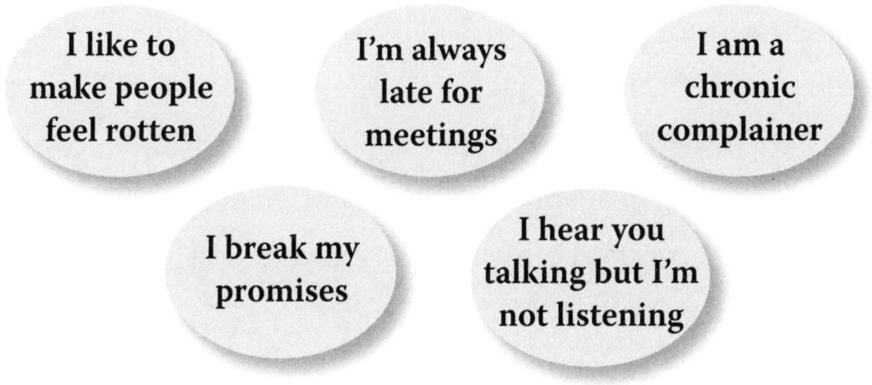

And A Million Other Messages

As I said before, you are setting an example for others to follow, whether you know it or not. Now, there are very few formal classes telling us about this big billboard we all carry around, and how well others can read our messages. So for the most part, it is our sole responsibility to be aggressive in scripting the messages we want others to read and hear.

The Good News

But, there is good news; even though you can't stop those daily broadcasts from happening, you can control your message. The key is to brand yourself before others begin to attach their own labels. Change those negative and self defeating messages before it's too late.

Leaders Lead

I have witnessed so called "leaders" who complain about how terrible the organization is- directly to their people. As a leader one of the first promises you make to your people (howbeit unspoken) is to provide the kind of leadership they can be proud of. I don't know anyone who wants to follow a bitter, frustrated, negative talking crybaby. People expect better from their leaders. We had a standing rule when I was in corporate America that we were to always pass negatives up, and positives down.

Remember, each day you encounter other people whether it is at home, at work, or in your community, you are setting an example and you are advertising your brand.

Promises Kept Inspire People

When you keep your promises to people, they get inspired. Because they believe you will keep your promises in the future. The same is true whether you are a parent in the home, or a CEO of a Fortune 500 company. Often times we only think of those so called "big promises" we make to people, but often it's the small promises that are broken that wear the team down.

For example:

- Those dreaded business meetings that always seem to run over in spite of the fact that employees were promised they would last only 30 minutes.
- Or your promise that problems in your Department, or organization would get your immediate attention, but one year later those problems still exist
- How about promises that the company would invest in new equipment and/or technology that will help increase employee productivity - but it somehow never happens.
- Or allowing certain people to continue to come late to work; after you promised employees at the last meeting things would be different.

Each time you break what you have promised to your people it diminishes your status as an effective leader. And when people begin to doubt your words - they begin to lose respect for you. So, as much as lies within your control, do what you promise.

Model Good Behavior

As I mentioned earlier, people often take on the traits of the leaders they follow. If you don't have the benefit of a person whom you feel has good habits, then seek out a person you admire and find out how they developed their winning ways.

A person who is successful when working with other people is a person who has worked hard, and continues to work hard at perfecting these skills. Yes; it's something you will have to continuously work at your whole life because you are dealing with the infinite variable- human beings. Humans are complex creatures who change quickly, and change often.

Who Are You Following

I heard someone once say that most people are like sheep, meaning they just follow the follower. In order to succeed you must learn to follow the leader, however, make sure that the person leading you is taking you where you want to go.

It's not complicated; if you want to be a happy person, then make it a point to associate with happy people. If you want get good at working with others, seek out those who are good at working with others. If you want to develop the type of character that gains the respect of the people you have to work with, live with, and do business with, then model those who have great character traits. Don't worry, in today's world these individuals won't be hard to find- just look round you. Every once in a while you'll meet a traveler on this high road. What are some of these great character traits you'll spot in these individuals?

- They have a warm smile that embraces others.
- They call other people's names with dignity.
- They are quick to at least listen to other's points of view.

- They never put down or demean others.
- They give others the benefit of the doubt.
- They go the extra mile (do more than is expected) in all that they do.
- They solicit the input and opinions of others, and take it into consideration.

It's No Fairytale

Some of you might say this sounds like a fairytale. It is for this very reason I say it won't be hard to spot these individuals. They are like aliens in today's society where it seems to be every man, woman, boy, and girl for themselves. The mantra of the day seems to be "make it by any means necessary," lie, cheat, and steal and no matter how many toes you have to step on, or how many promises you break; all is fair in love and war - right?

Here is a powerful saying. I don't know who was the very first person to say this. Since thoughts have been around for centuries, but whoever was the first- had to have some real life experiences when they said:

Be careful how you treat people on the way up...because you'll going to meet those same people on the way down.

-Anonymus

Whether you are just starting your career or you're renewing your commitment to learning how to get along with people, you must establish yourself as a person of your word. No, I'm not saying we are perfect, but everyday you should be striving to be better and do better than the day before.

You Have the Keys

Well, there you have it; the *7 People Principles: Success When Dealing With Other People.* Now go back and not only read these principals, but study them one by one. In them you will find your golden keys to the kingdom.

Thank You

I want to personally thank you for allowing me to share this space and time with you, I truly enjoyed our visit. One last note; while I was finishing this book (in the early A.M) I recalled being asked by one of my students just yesterday, if I really believe in these principles? My reply was - absolutely. I have lived every one of these principles first hand as you can tell by the cases I have cited.

One of the things I realized early in my career was this: if I was to truly succeed in life- I had to learn how to get along with people. I have made the study of people my life's work. One of the questions I sought answers to as a young child, born in the ghettos of east Dallas, was "what makes successful people succeed?" What I found out, was; one of the primary reasons people succeed at the highest levels in our society is this: THEY HAVE LEARNED HOW TO SUCESSFULLY WORK WITH OTHER PEOPLE!

It is a fact of life that no matter how much money you make, and no matter how talented you are, if you can't get along with others you are a failure. Because no matter where you go in life, you are bound to run into PEOPLE!

Lessons Learned

Can you list three ideas you picked in this chapter that will help you have success when dealing with other people.

Write your answers here:

1. ____

____

____.

2. ____

____

____.

3. ____

____

____.

What follows next is a bonus Chapter that I wanted you to have... I won't tell you what is in there. It's a surprise you'll have to see for yourself. So let's go there now...

People Principal #7:

“People Want You to
Do What You Promise”

CHAPTER EIGHT

Bonus Chapter

Motivating the Plateaued Employee

For a number of reasons an employee may reach a level where their personal performance has peaked, leveled, or fallen off precipitously and they no longer are contributing to the success of the company or team. The question then becomes: how do you coach this individual back to excellent performance? Here are a list of strategies I believe will help reengage the employee, so both the company and employee benefits greatly from increased productivity.

Why Employees Plateau

The list is endless as to the reasons an employee's performance peaks and begins to fall off. For a salesperson: perhaps they have lost confidence in themselves, the company, or the product they are selling. For an executive: it may be that they have reached a level of incompetence and now feel overwhelmed (e.g. the Peter Principle). A person nearing retirement may feel they have been marginalized, and now they no longer want to contribute to the success of the team. Still another employee, leaving for a new position inside or outside of the organization, may feel they no longer need to give their best efforts. This list can go on and on; but one underlining question remains - How do you reengage these individuals?

Legitimate Question

This question of inspiring employees back to excellent performance is nothing new to me. While serving in the military, I had the honor of being named "Sailor of the Quarter" at this particular command based on performance, productivity, and professionalism. I was then nominated for "Sailor of the Year" at the same command. When I came before the selection board (made up of seven senior officers and senior enlisted men and women), I was asked one question I've pondered and had to navigate my entire career. "How do you motivate a person whose performance has "plateaued" in the organization? This is a legitimate question in any organization; be it government, for profit, non-profit, a corporation, small business, even an organization made up of volunteers.

First Things Fast

As a performance technologist, working with organizations, my first step, is to conduct a front end or needs assessment of the organization. The idea here is to uncover what the organization wants to accomplish as a whole, hence, what they need. This includes a thorough review of the company's mission statement and an evaluation of how each department is supporting the overall mission.

What Do Employees Know?

If this process works for a company, the same will work when assessing individual performance. First, I'd like to find out if the employee knows and understands the overall mission of the organization. A sad fact is more often than not, employees haven't a clue as to the overall mission of the company. And if they were ever briefed on the mission at all, they have long since forgotten what it is.

Well, as I've said before, it is hard to get excited about anything you don't understand. And just like we assess the needs of the organization; the organization needs to assess the needs of its employees. One entity that does this better than others is sales organizations.

Driven To Succeed

High octane sales organizations keep their hand on the pulse of their sales forces. Here are several things they do very well:

1. They are masters at getting their people to understand the overall mission of the company (e.g. in the next five years we will be the number one company in our industry).

2. They are great at helping their people understand exactly where they fit in the grand scheme of things e.g. (the support department's job is critical because our sales force depends on us to get the products to our customers in a timely and professional manner).
3. They are excellent at getting their people to understand how each and every individual, and the jobs they are assigned, directly impacts how the mission will be accomplished (e.g. your job in accounting is to make sure the sales force is paid in a timely manner, and that their paychecks are correct).

Each team member's role is clearly defined; and they understand the direct impact they have on accomplishing the mission. Show me an organization that employs these strategies, and I'll show you an organization that annihilates its competition.

Have a One-on-One

So, in a nutshell: the first step to motivating a "plateaued" employee is to have a one-on-one with them, and reiterate with them, the overall mission of the company. Second, help them understand the exact role they play in accomplishing the mission. And remember, everyone wants to feel they are a part of something special and that their contributions matter.

Pseudo Psychologist?

In order to motivate "plateaued" employees, you must get into their heads and try to understand why the employee has stopped contributing to the success of the organization. There is always the reason they give, and then - there is the real reason. Your mission is to uncover the real reason. Companies are good at telling employees what they need and expect. But turn around is fair play. In conducting an individual needs analysis or assessment of the employee, you want to find out directly from them, "what do you need or expect from your relationship with the company?"

For example, if they are leaving for a new position in four weeks and they have stopped contributing to the success of the mission, ask what they need and expect in those coming weeks? If they are retiring in six months, ask what they need and expect from the company during those last six months? And when coaching the employee whose production levels have peaked, ask them what they need and expect from the company in order to help them return to acceptable levels of performance. They may need some refresher training courses, or you may have to get them into some team training.

The key is to engage the employee and get them to talk to you. So, my advice to companies is simple - ask. "Ask and you shall receive." Ask the right questions, and they'll help unlock the mystery of the plateaued employee and lead you to drafting a rehabilitation plan for that employee. This is not to say what the employee needs or expects will be granted, but at least the company is operating from a position of knowledge and not operating in the dark. With this knowledge, both the employer and the employee can decide whether the two of them can continue to work together.

Final Exultation

Repetition is the key to rapid learning. Now, go back and look at the notes you took throughout this book. Then re-read the areas of importance to you and begin to put these strategies in place. Finally, believe you can make a difference in the lives of people.

Catch me on the internet at www.cubieking.com. Or
www.goldcrowninc.com or, look for me live in your city.
Until next time...go out there and...

Make Your Dreams King!

References

Anthony, R. (1973). Advanced formula for total success. New York: NY: Berkley Books.

Blanchard, K. & Johnson, S (1981). The one minute manager. New York,NY: Berkley Books.

Bristol, C.M. (1948). The magic of believing. Englewood, NJ: Pocket Books.

Carnegie, D. (1936). How to win friends and influence people. New York, NY: Simon and Schuster.

Chevalier, R. (2004). Human performance technology revisited. Silver Spring, MD: International Society for Performance Improvement.

Covey, S.R. (1989). The 7 habits of highly effective people. New York: Simon & Schuster.

Douglas, M.R. (1966). How to make a habit of succeeding. Grand Ripids, MI: Zondervan Books.

Hill, N. (1960). Think & grow rich: New York: Ballantine Books.

Holton, E.F.III. (1996). *The flawed four-level evaluation model.* Human Resource Development Quarterly, 7(1), pp. 23-25.

Rummler, G.A., & Brache, A.P. (1995). Improving performance: How to manage the white space on the organization chart (2nd.Ed.). San Francisco, CA: Jossey-Bass.

Skinner, B.F. (1953). Beyond freedom and dignity. NewYork: Random House.

Skinner, B.F. (1974). About behaviorism. NewYork: Random House.

Swanson, R. A., & Holton, E.F. (1997).(Eds.). Human resource development research handbook.

San Francisco, CA: Berrett-Koehler Publishers.

Williams, A. (1984). Pushing up people. Doraville, GA: Parklake Publishing

About The Author

Dr. Cubie Davis King

Dr. Cubie Davis King is an internationally known performance technologist with a PhD. in training, performance, and improvement.

Known as "The King of Inspiration," he is a 9 year Navy Veteran of the U. S. Military. His storied career includes 4 yeas as a contracts negotiator for the Department of Defense, and a combined 12 years as an executive with Xerox and CitiGroup.

Dr. King has written 10 books, and authored over 60 articles dealing with performance and productivity. His life's work has been to coach and inspire people to new levels of peak performance in life and in business. He has donated his time to inner city youth programs, and spent time as a volunteer instructor going into middle schools inspiring youths through the National Jr. Achievement program. He has also volunteered his time to be a success and life coach for high school students.

Dr King has been recognized as a top producer at every place he has worked; starting with his nine years in the military, his years at the Department of Defense, at Xerox, and CitiGroup. Dr. King knows what motivates employees to move beyond the ordinary and reach new levels of productivity, having done it himself.

He now travels the world as a keynote and breakout speaker; working with governments on all levels (city, state, and federal), small businesses, non-profits, and corporations. Dr. King brings a unique approach to inspiring people to high achievements and sustained productivity.

To book Dr. King for your next meeting, go directly to his websites: www.goldcrowninc.com and www.cubieking.com, or or email him directly at cubie@goldcrowninc.com.

Notes

Notes

Notes

Notes